40 Relaxing Kaleidoscopes To Color
Adult Coloring Book

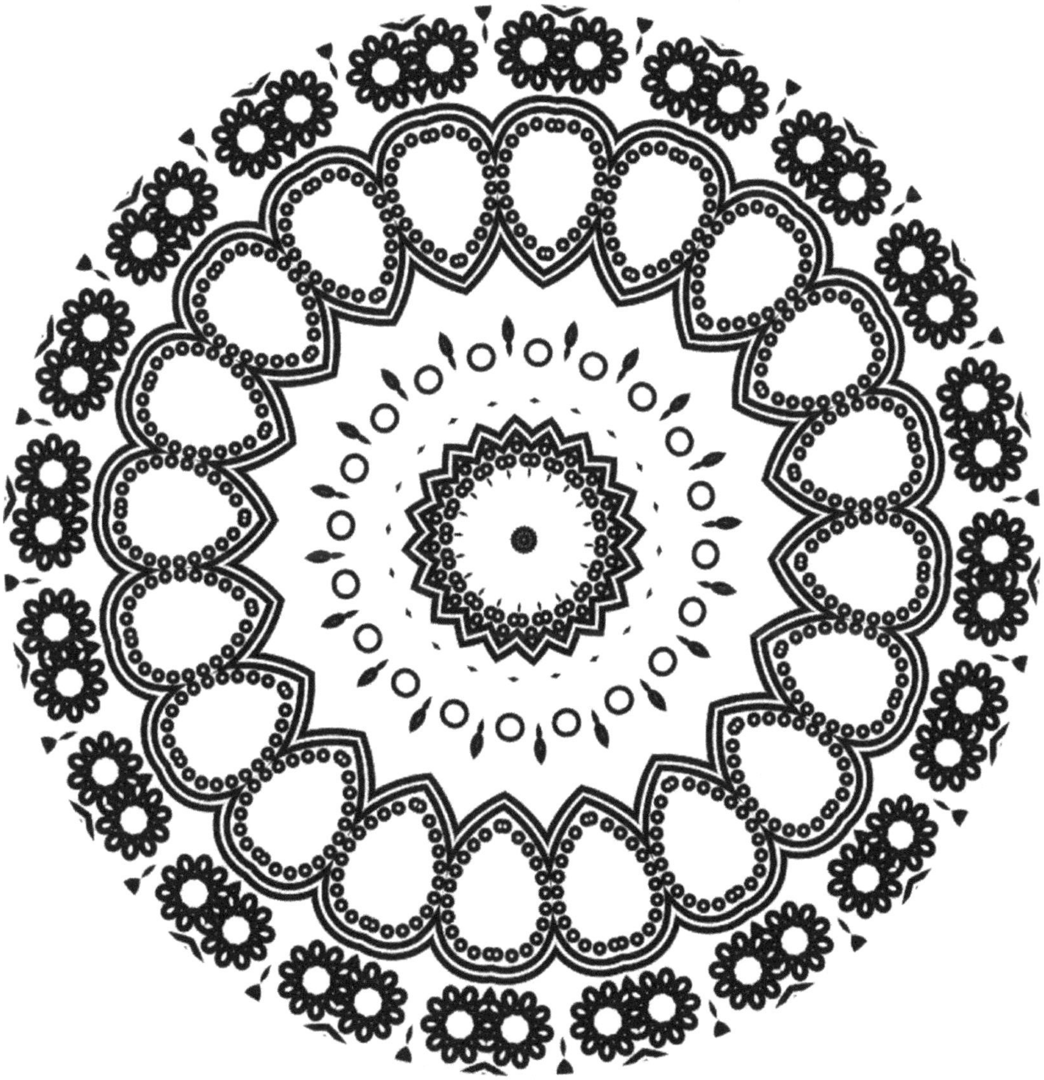

This belongs to:

____

____

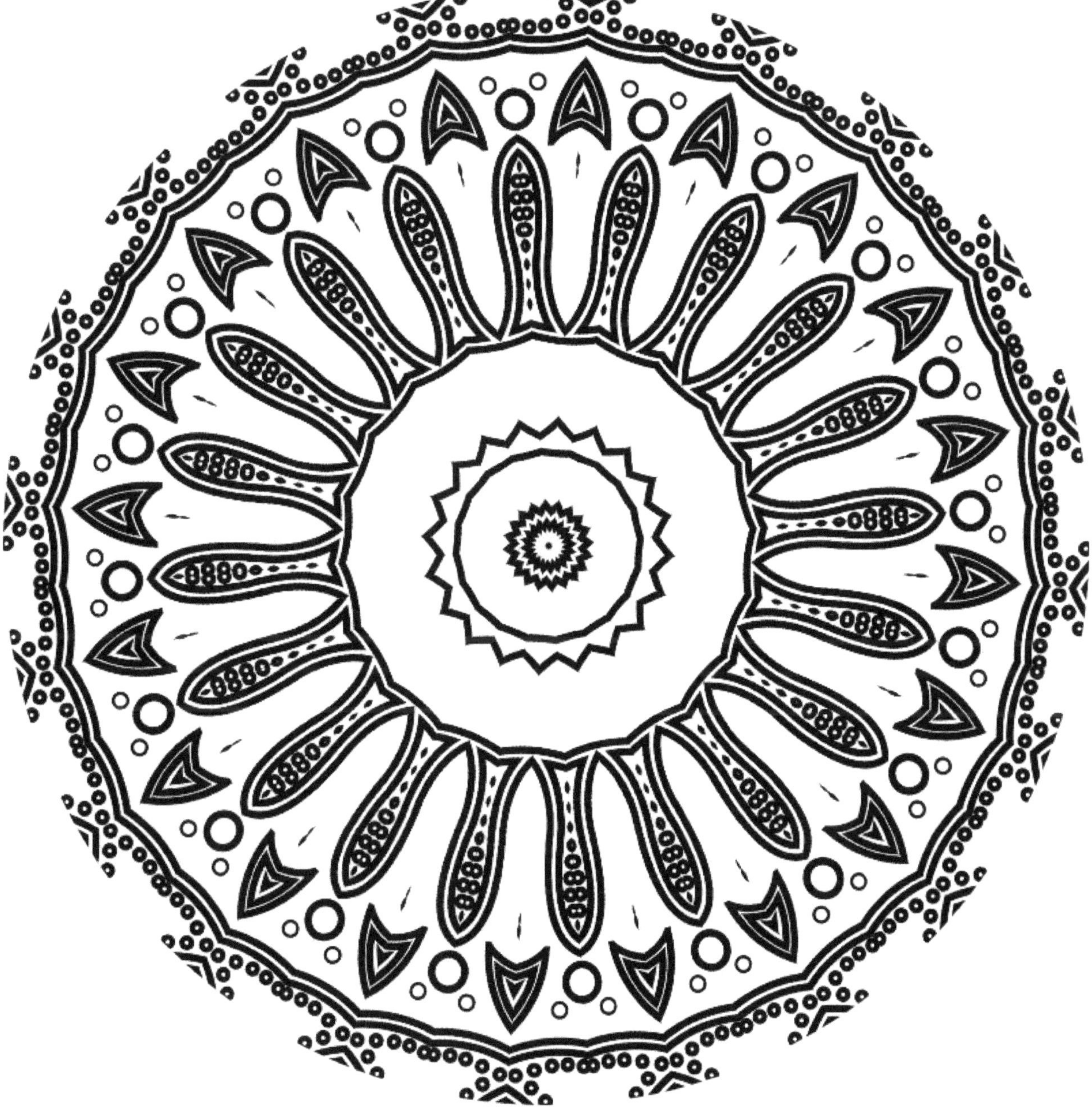

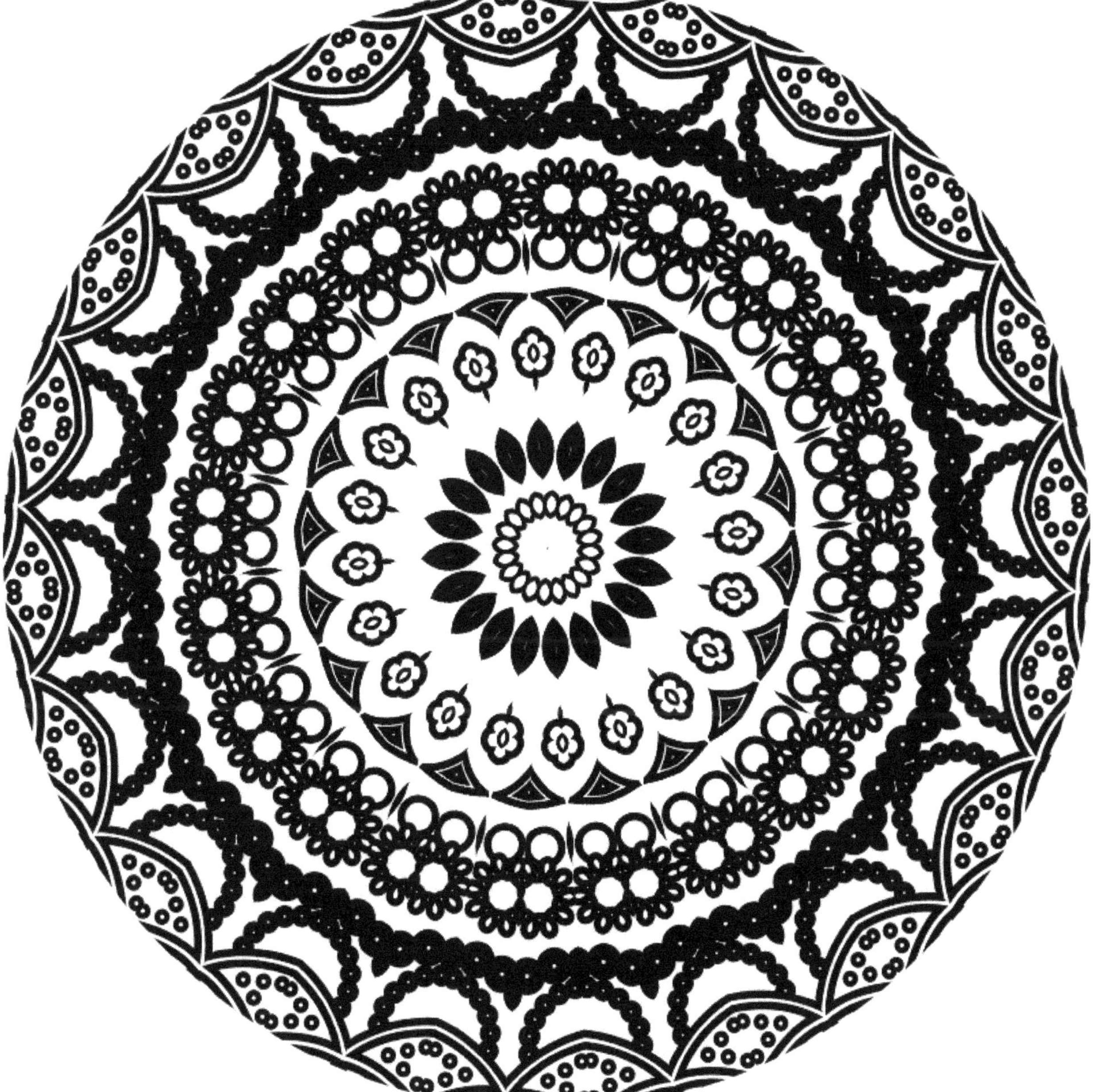

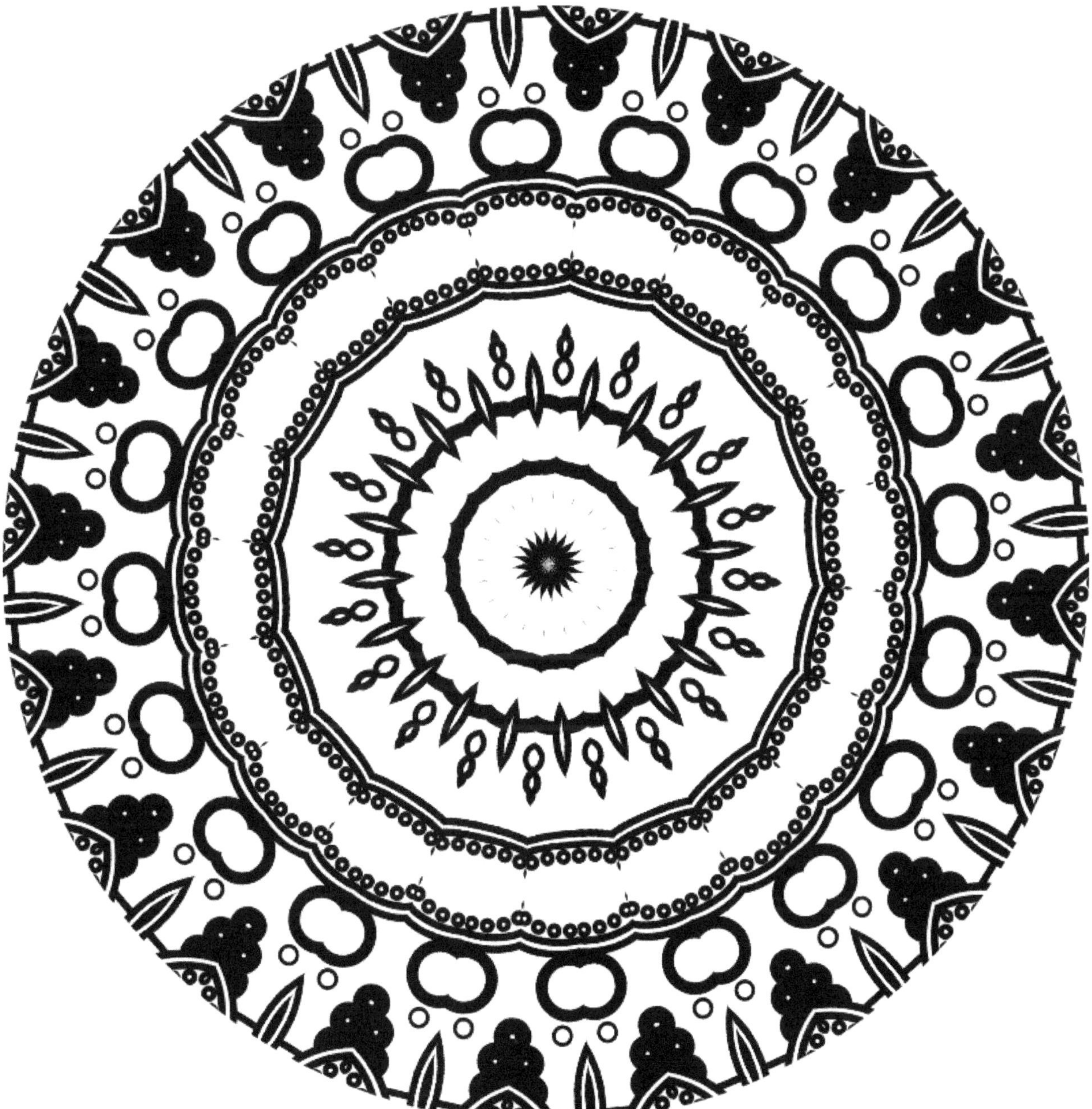

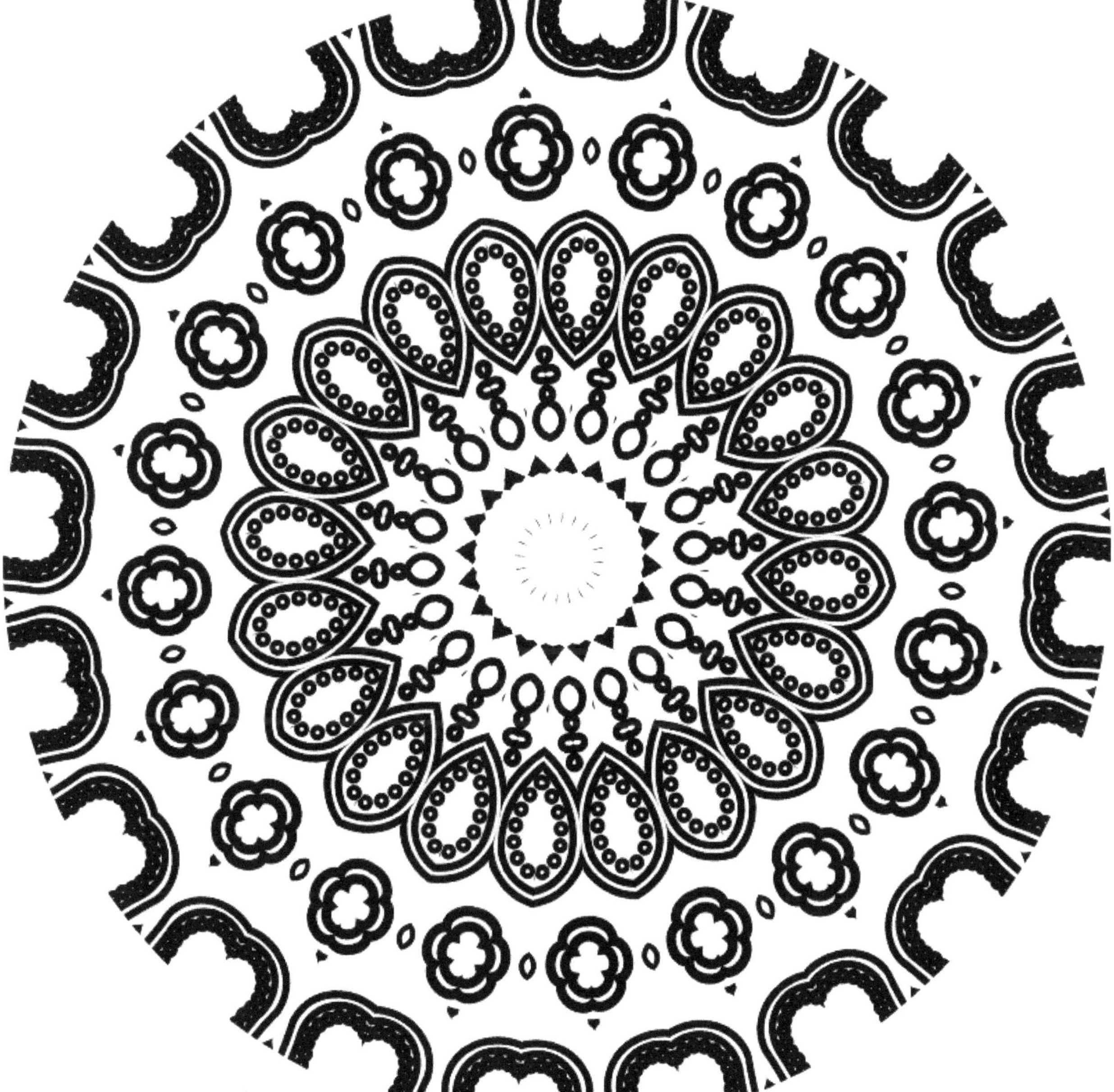

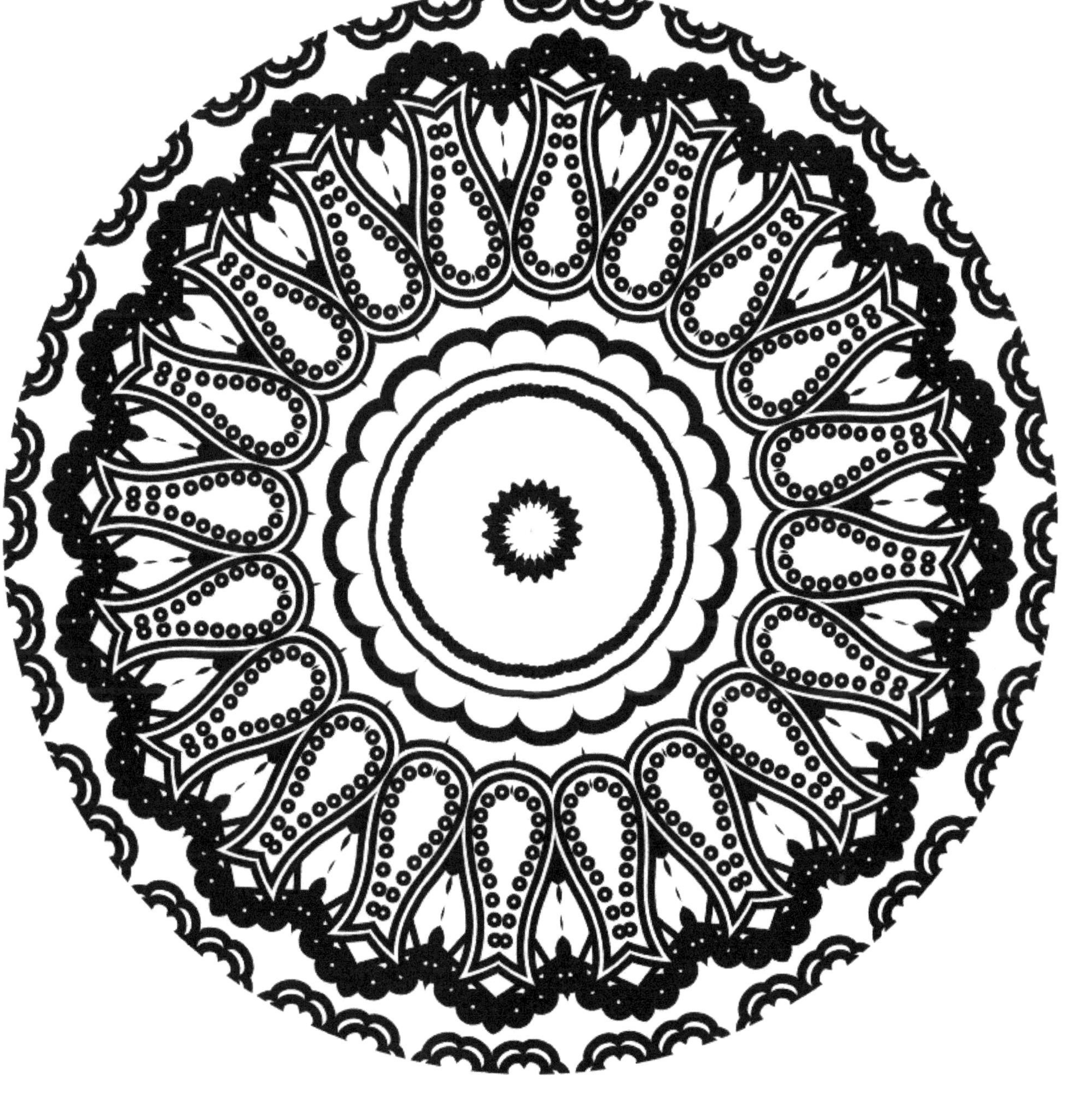

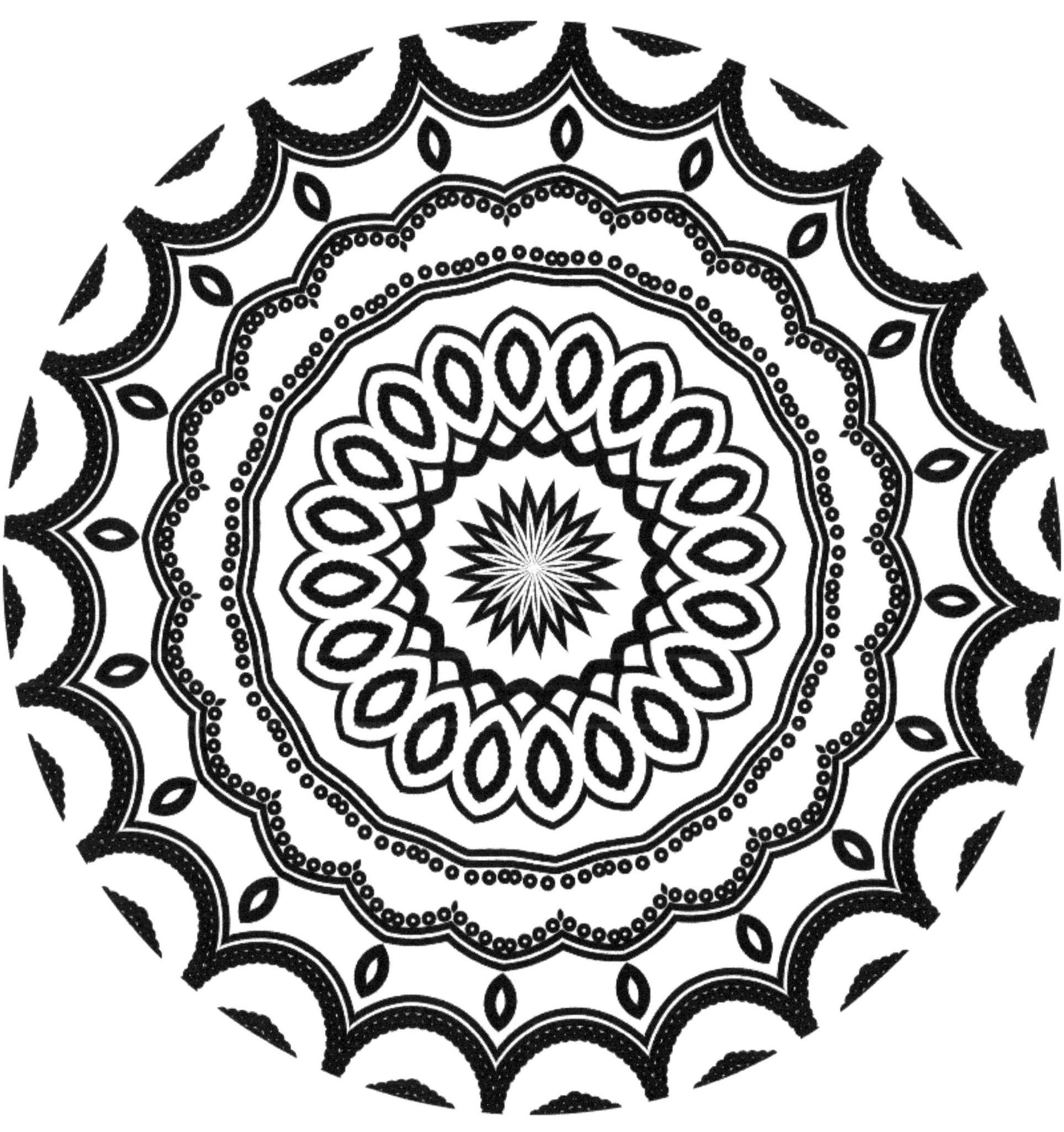

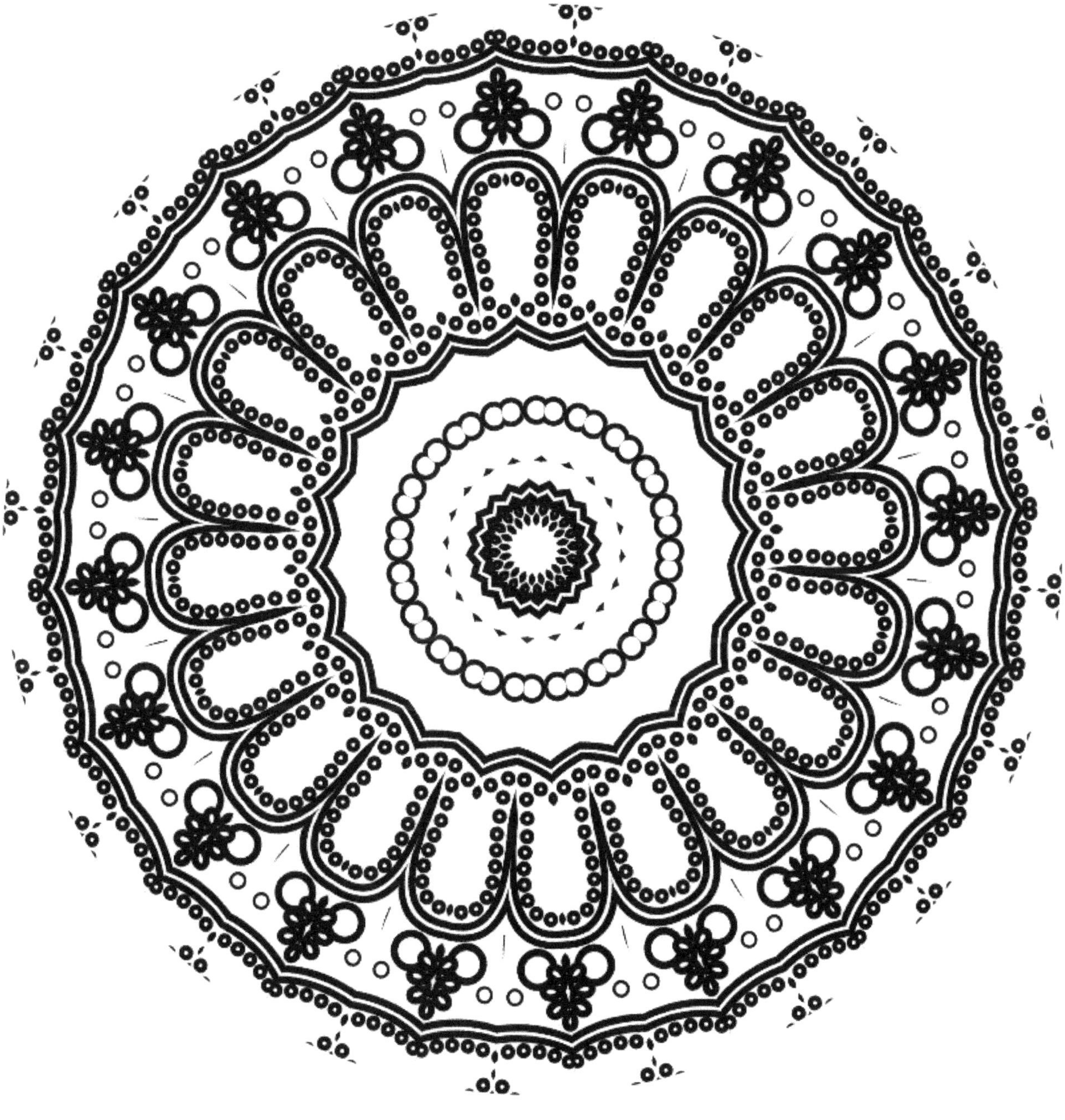

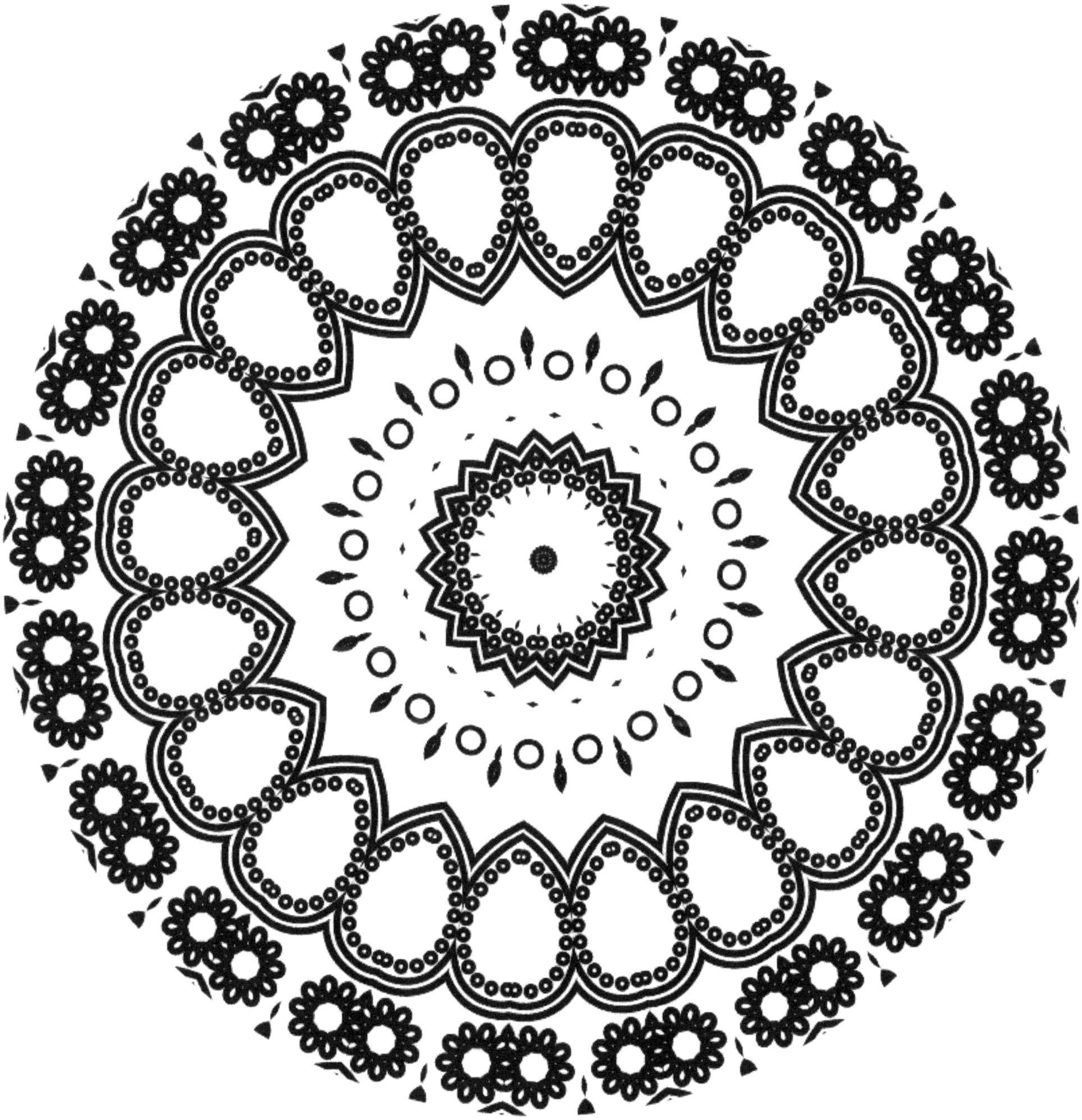

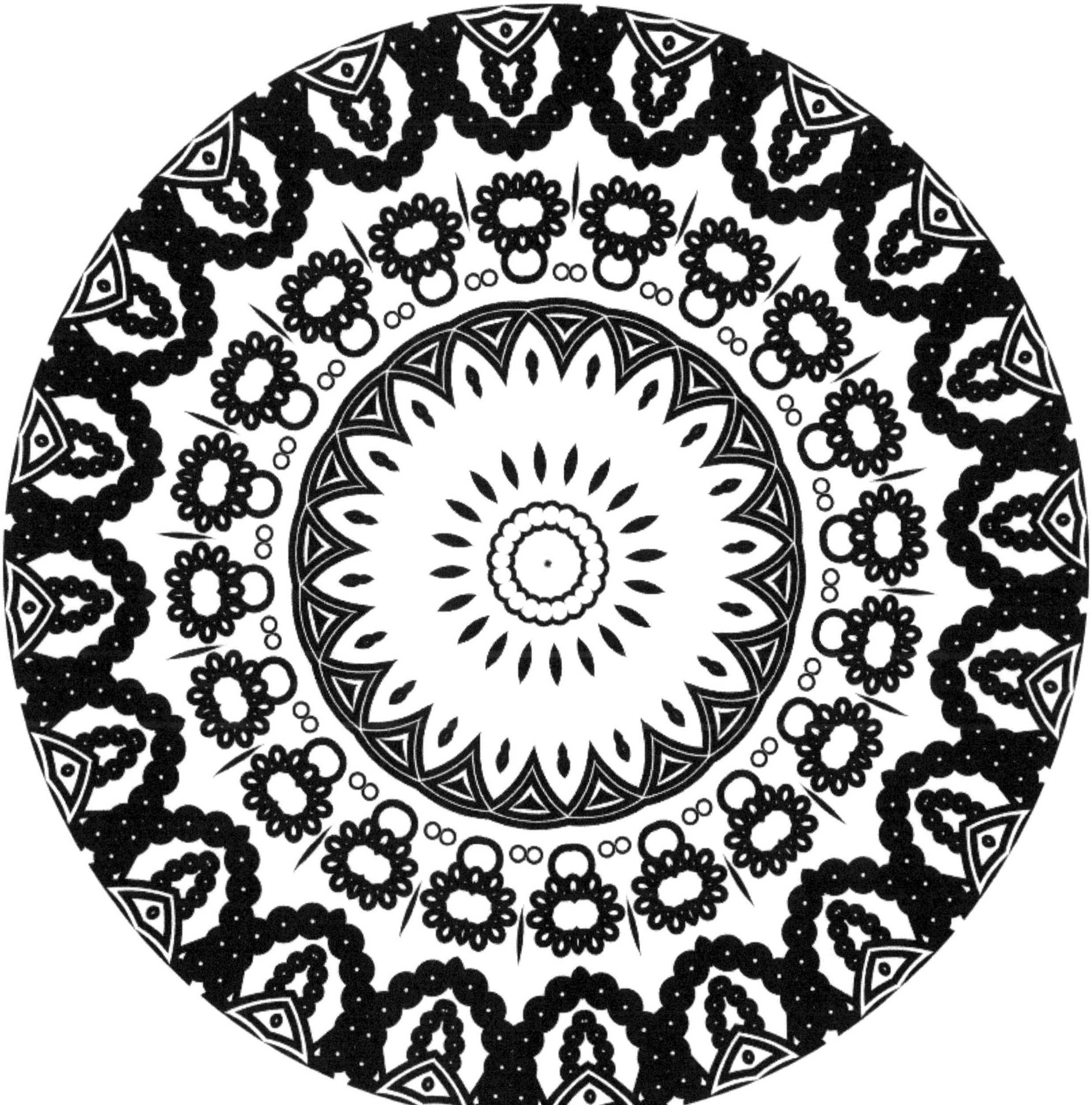

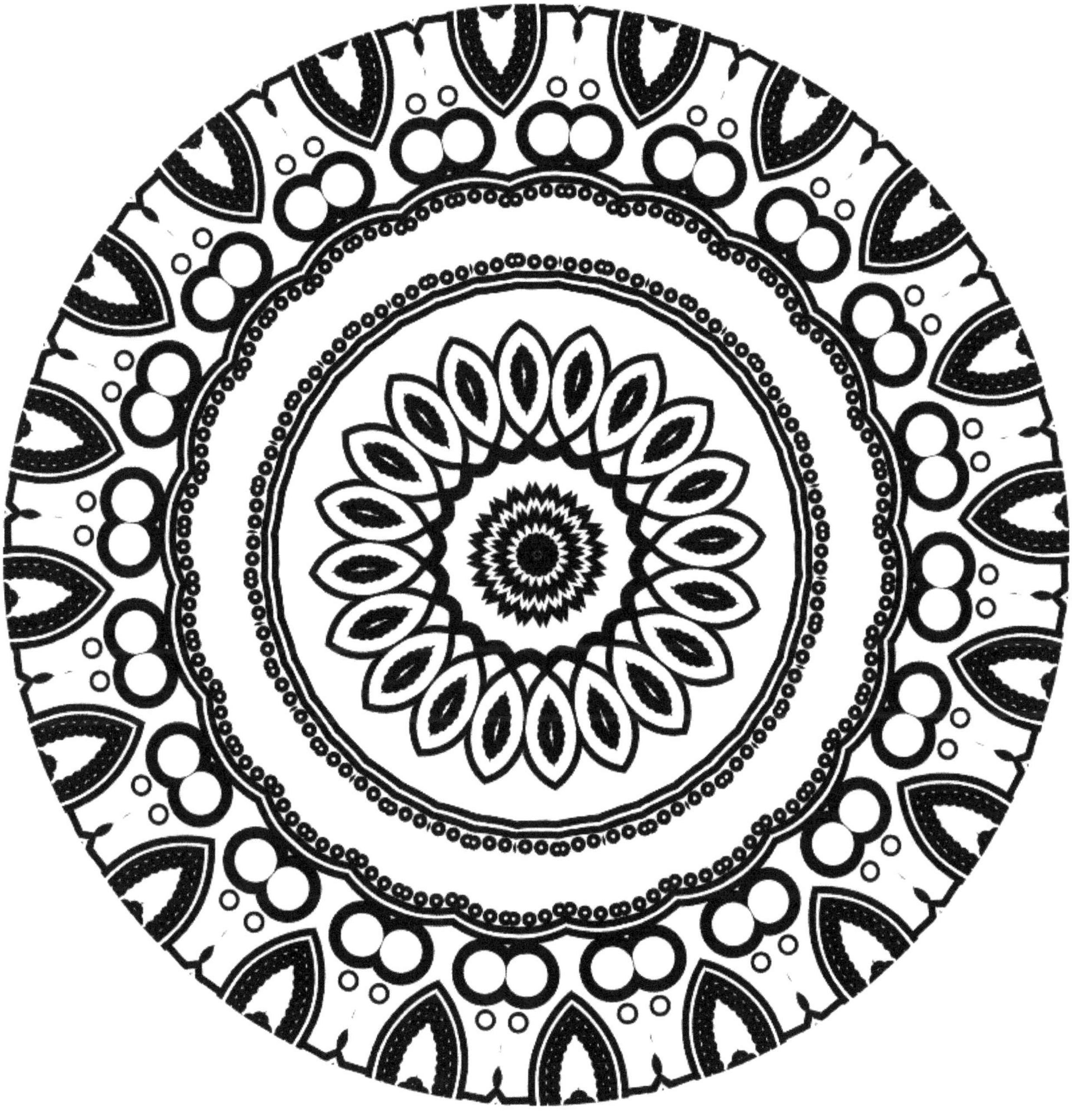

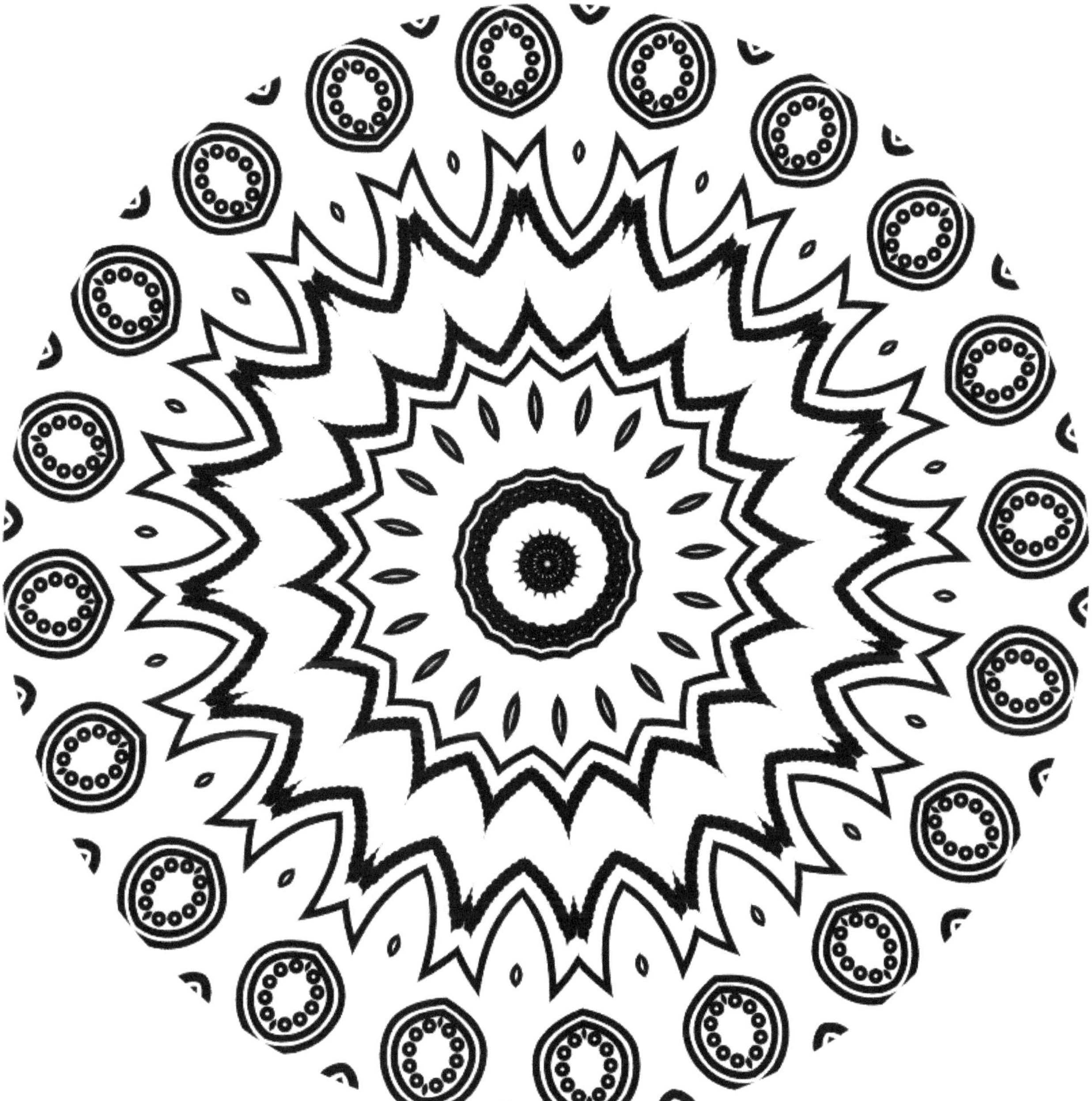

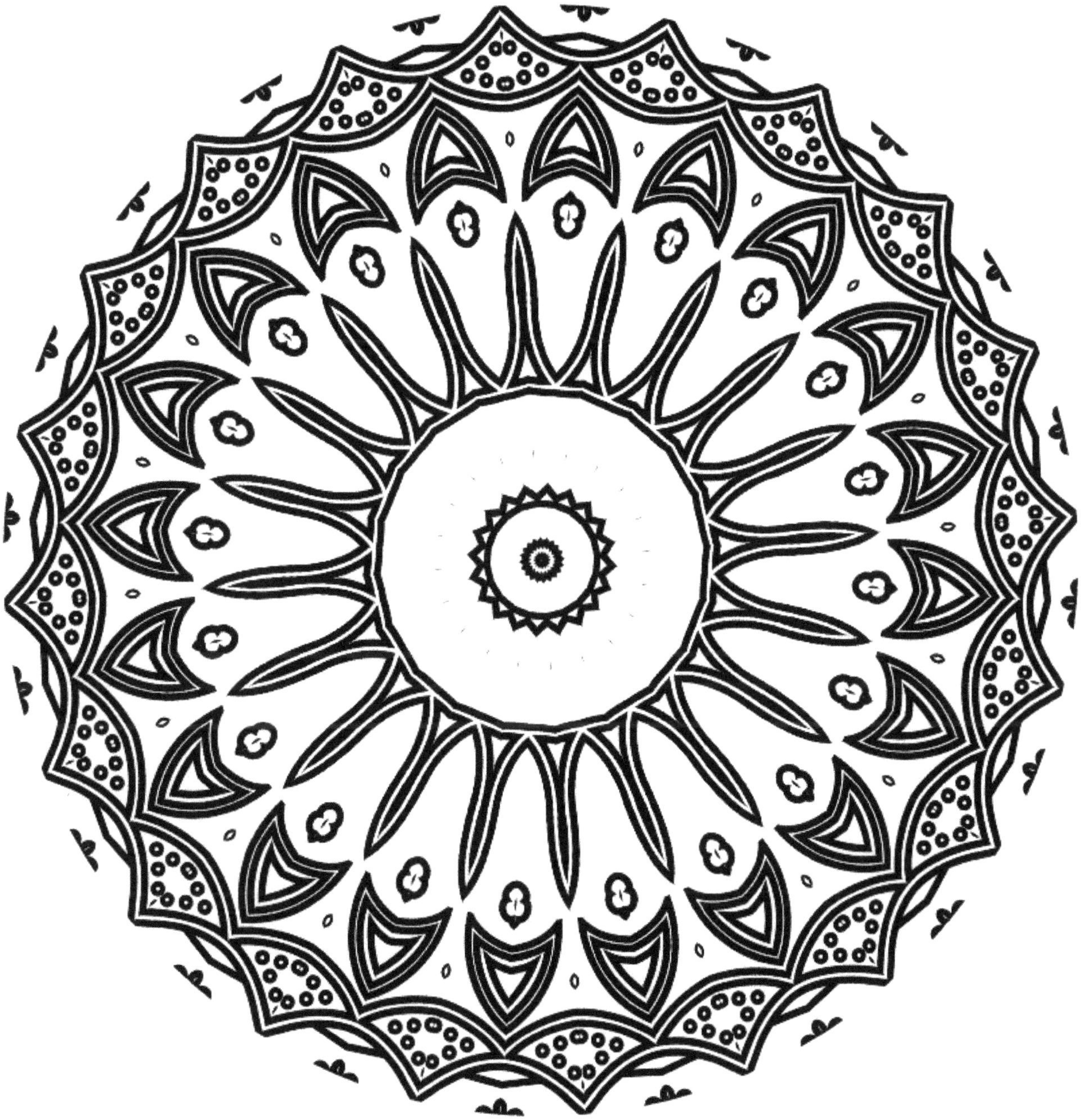

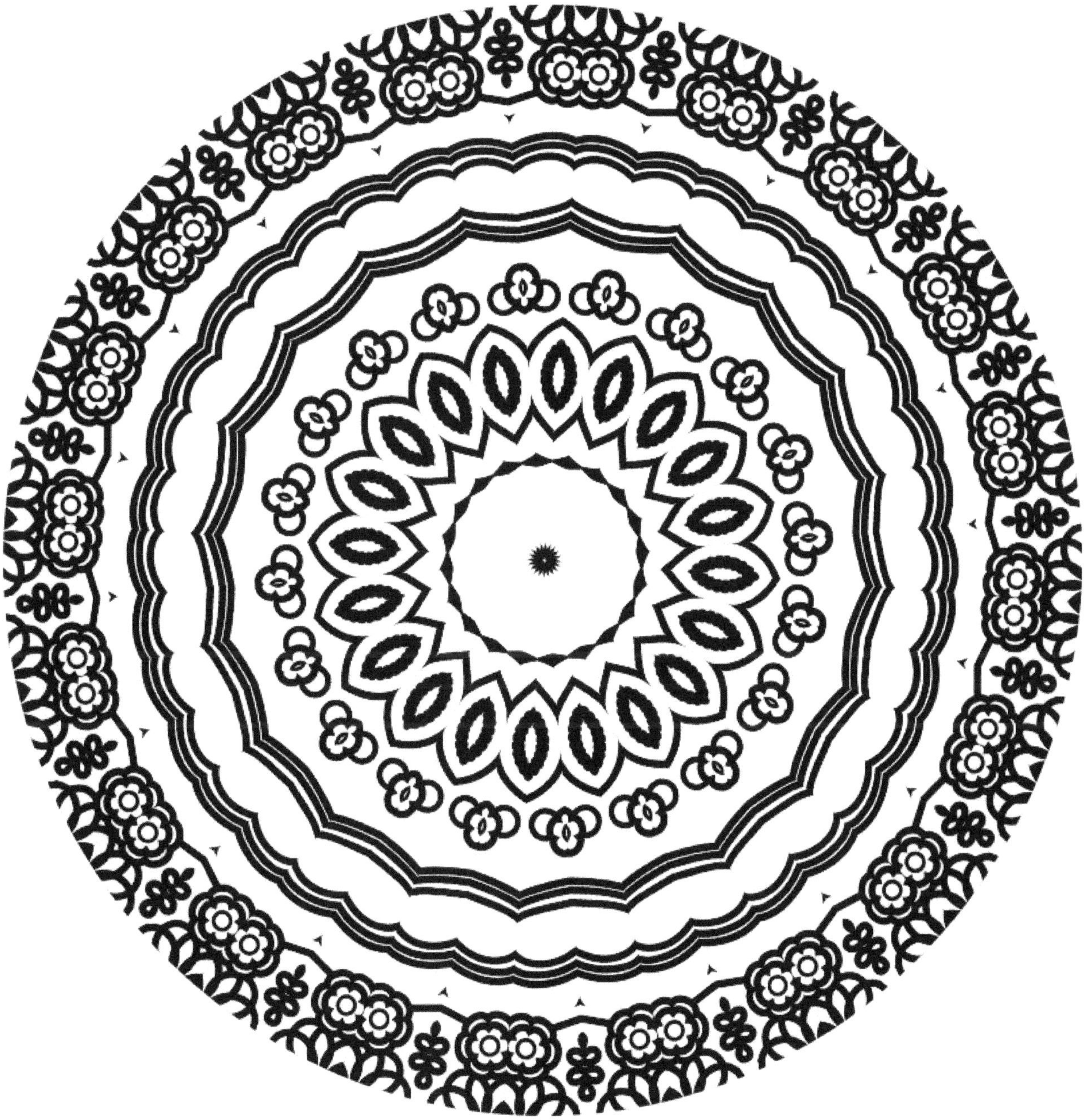

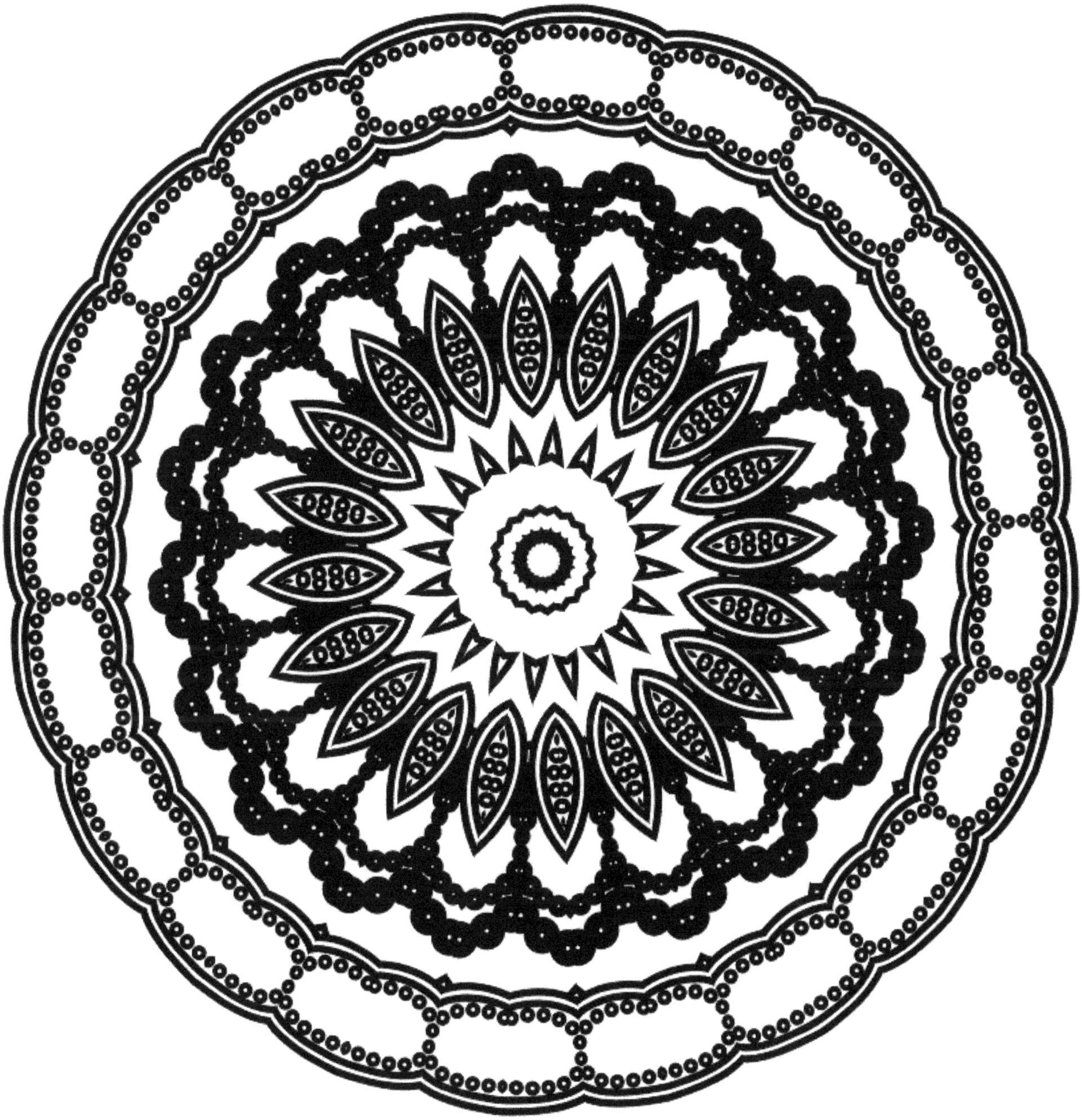

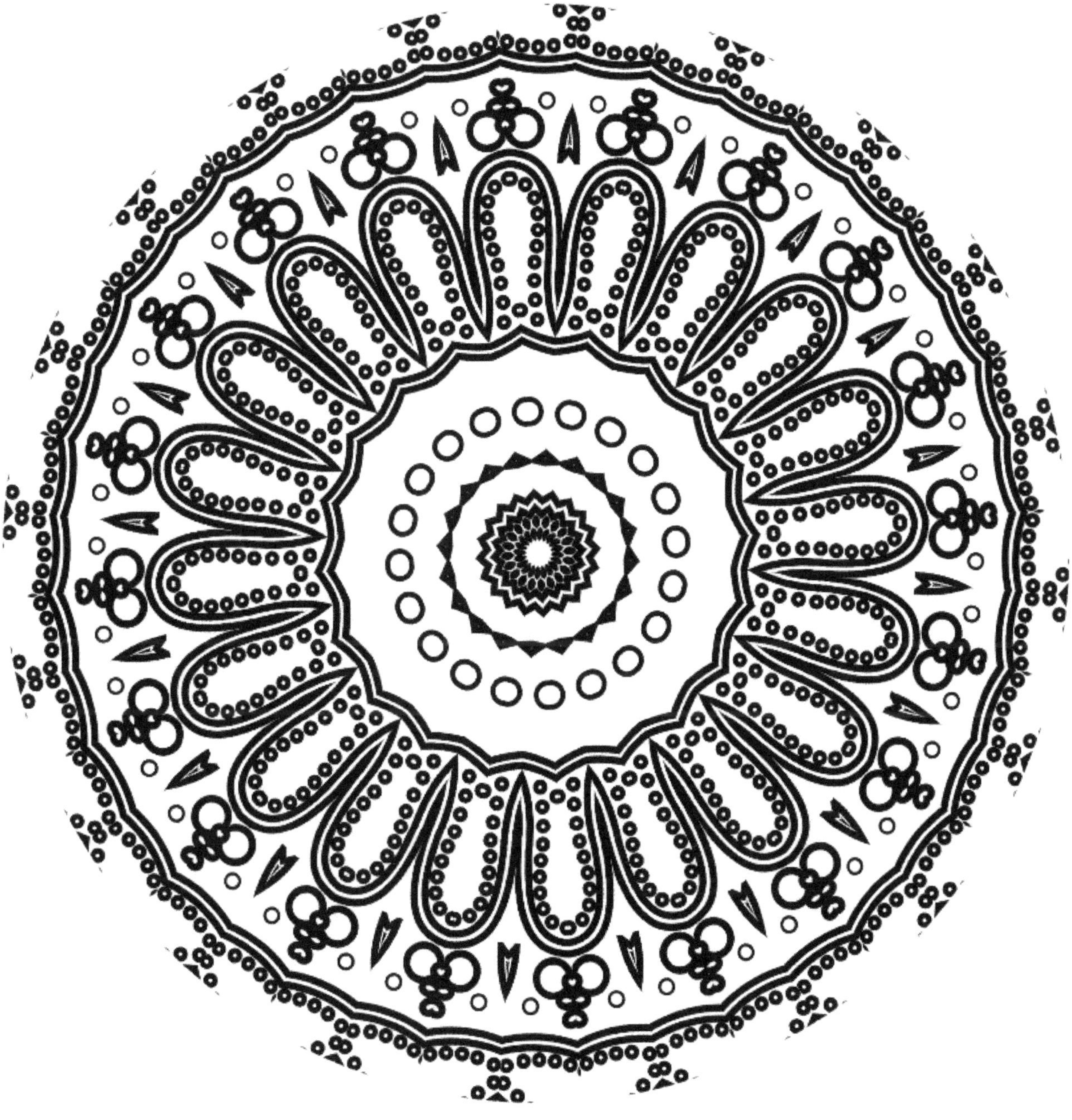

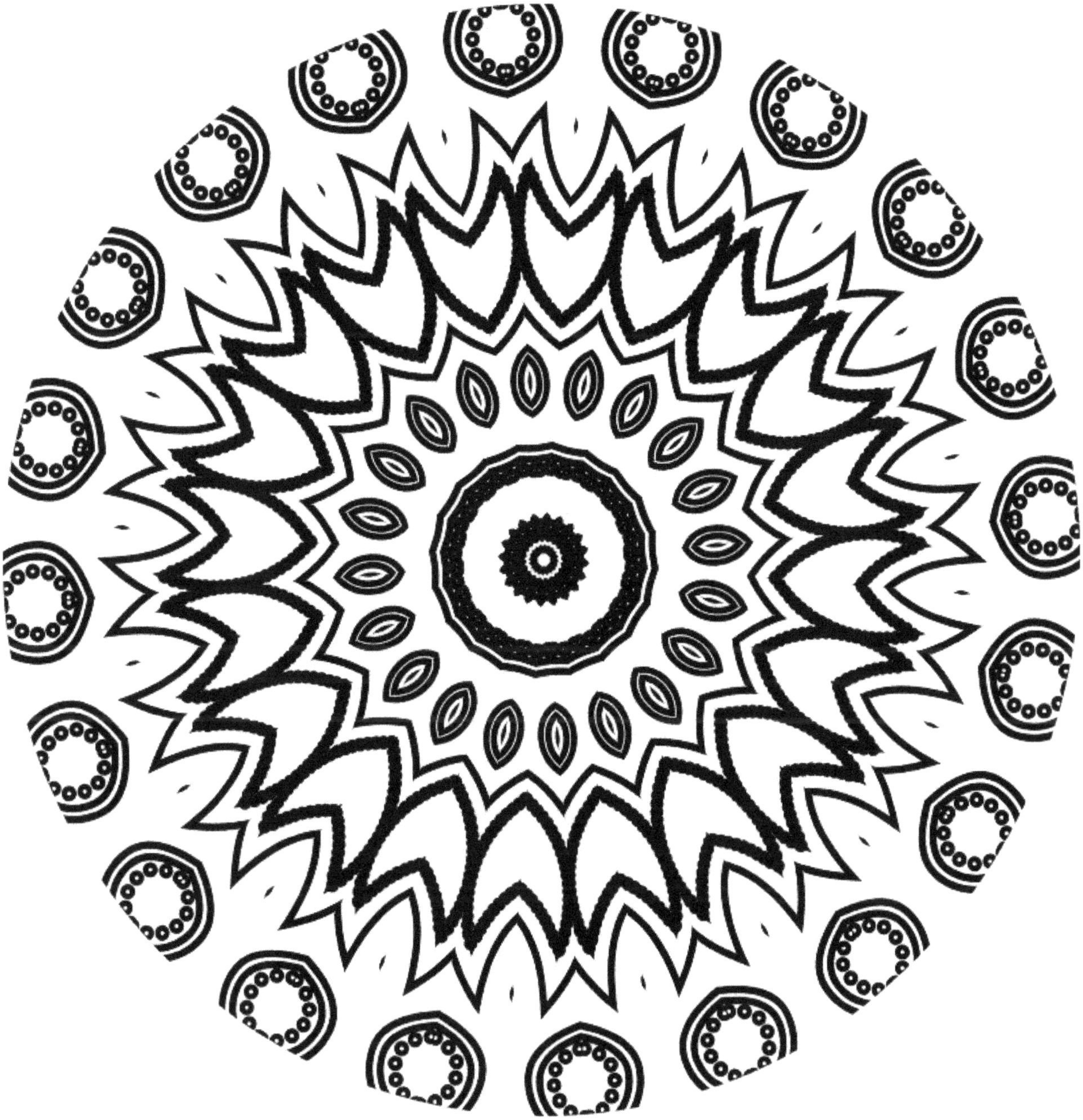

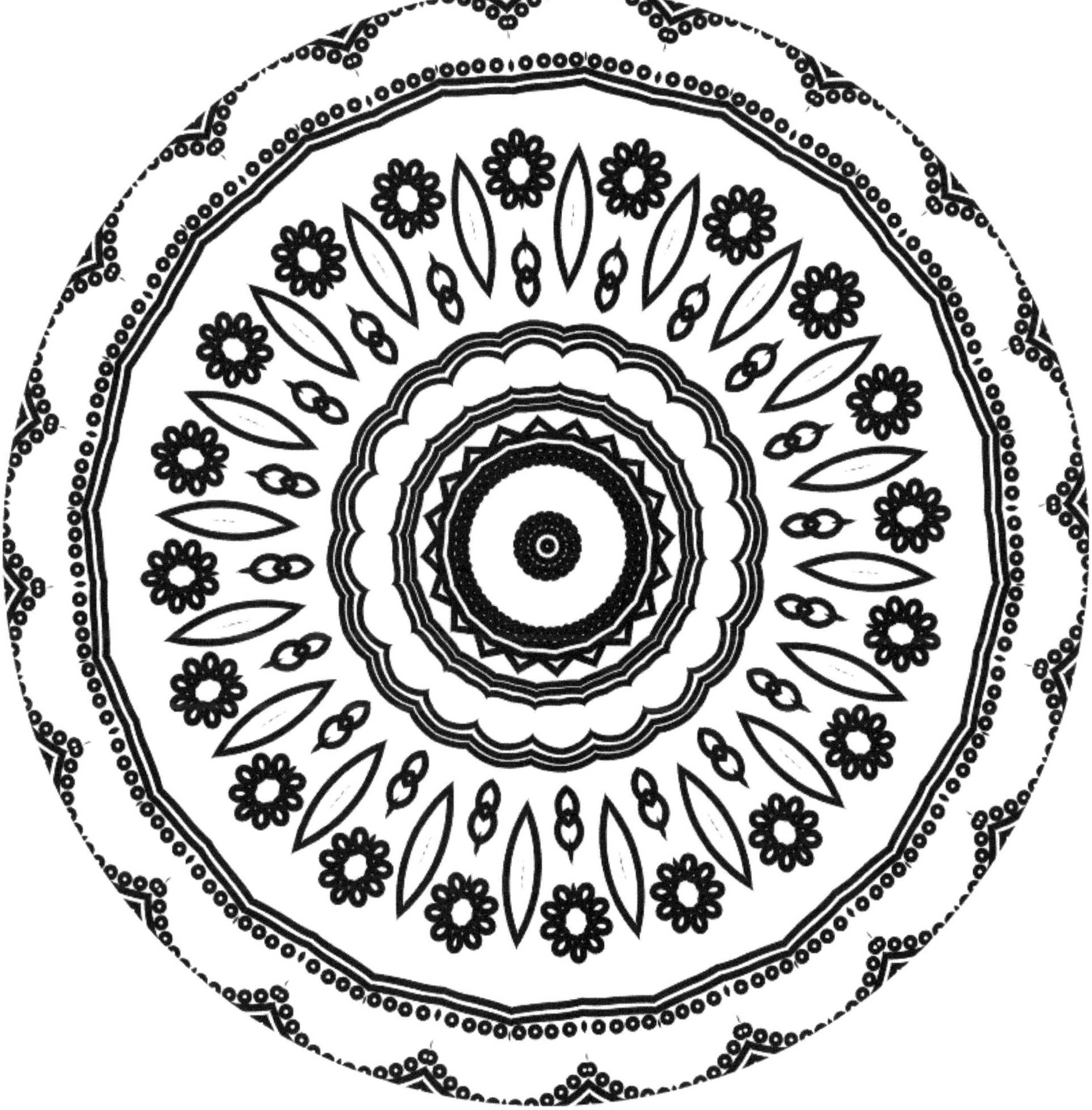

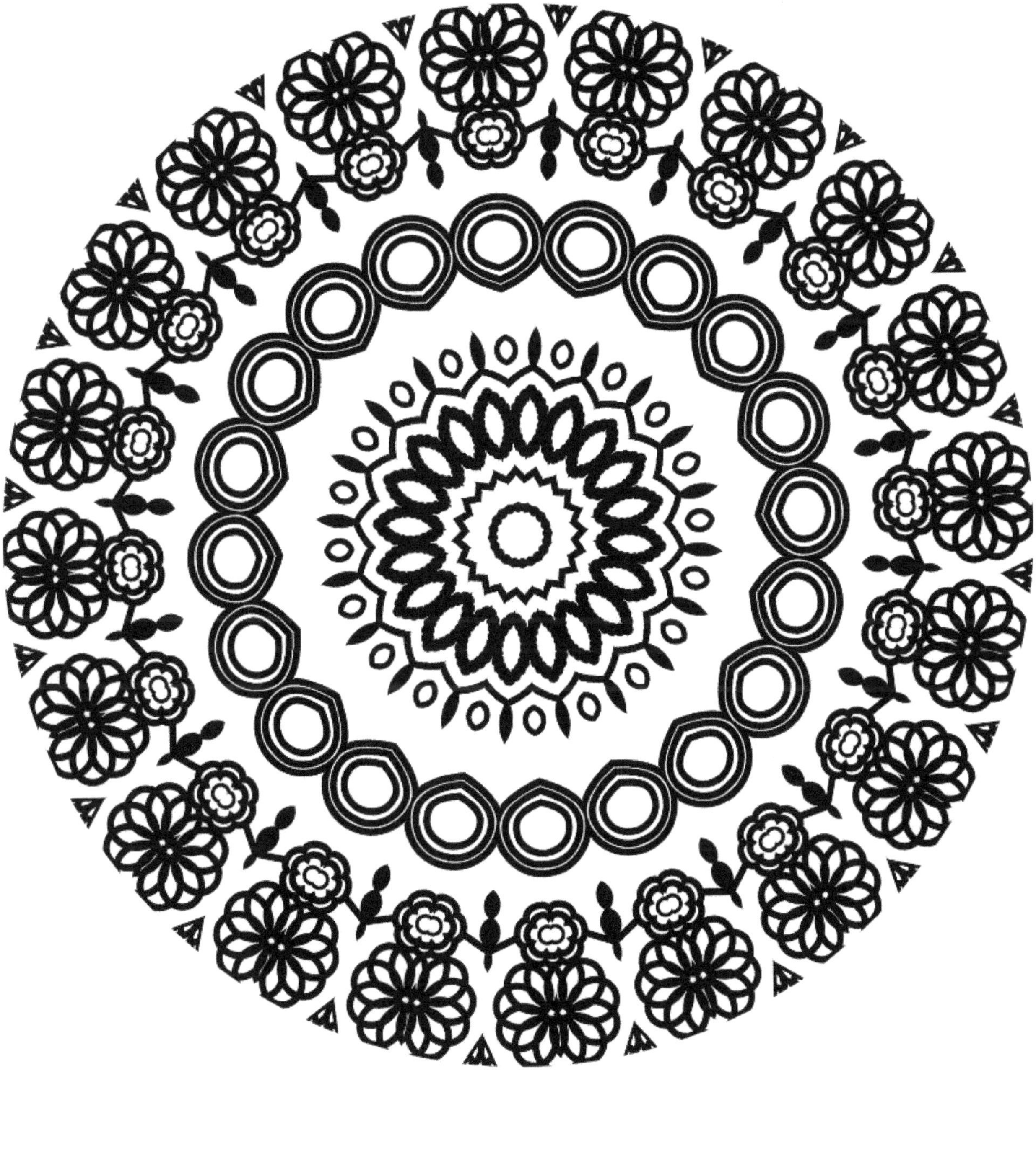

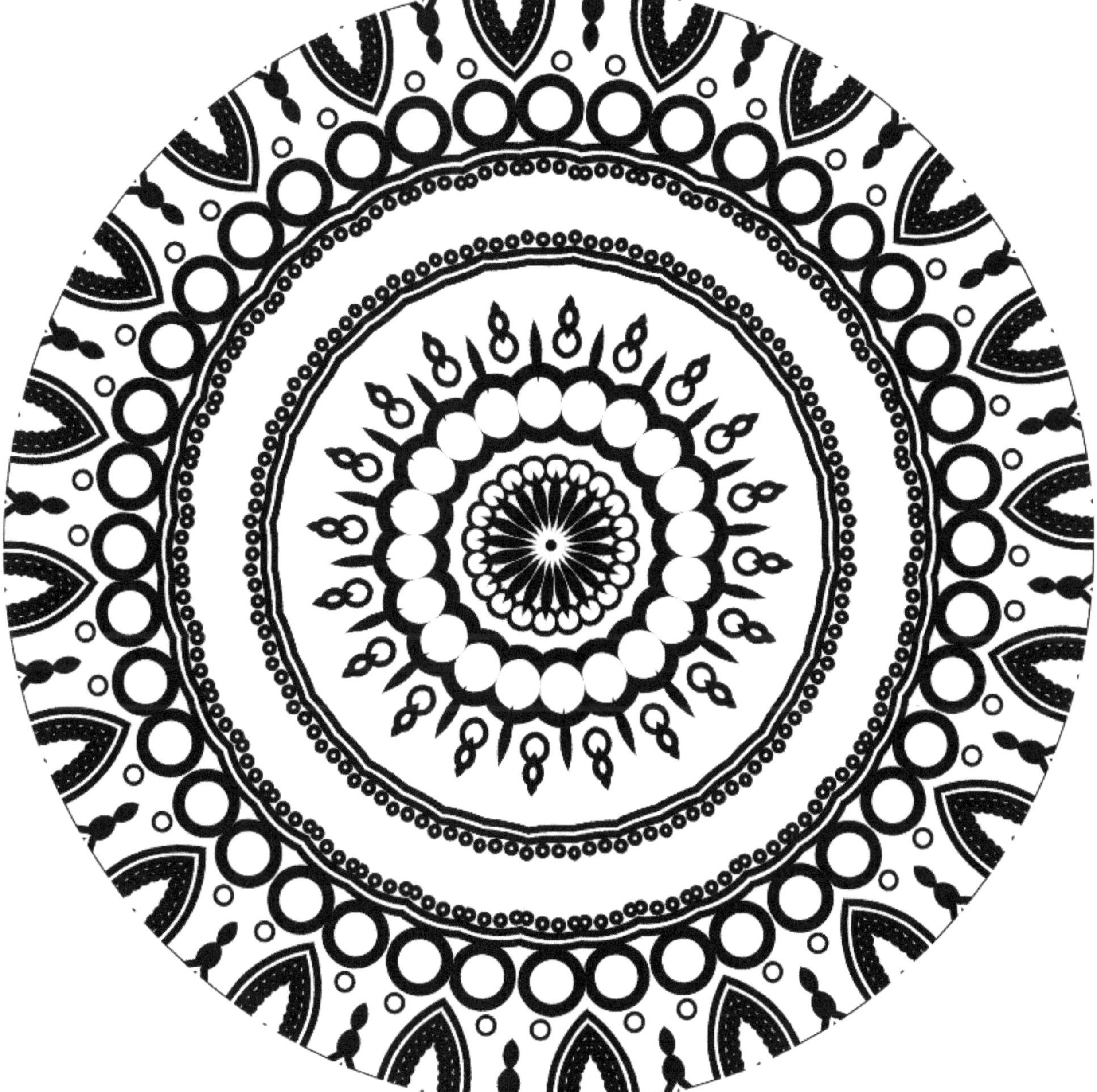

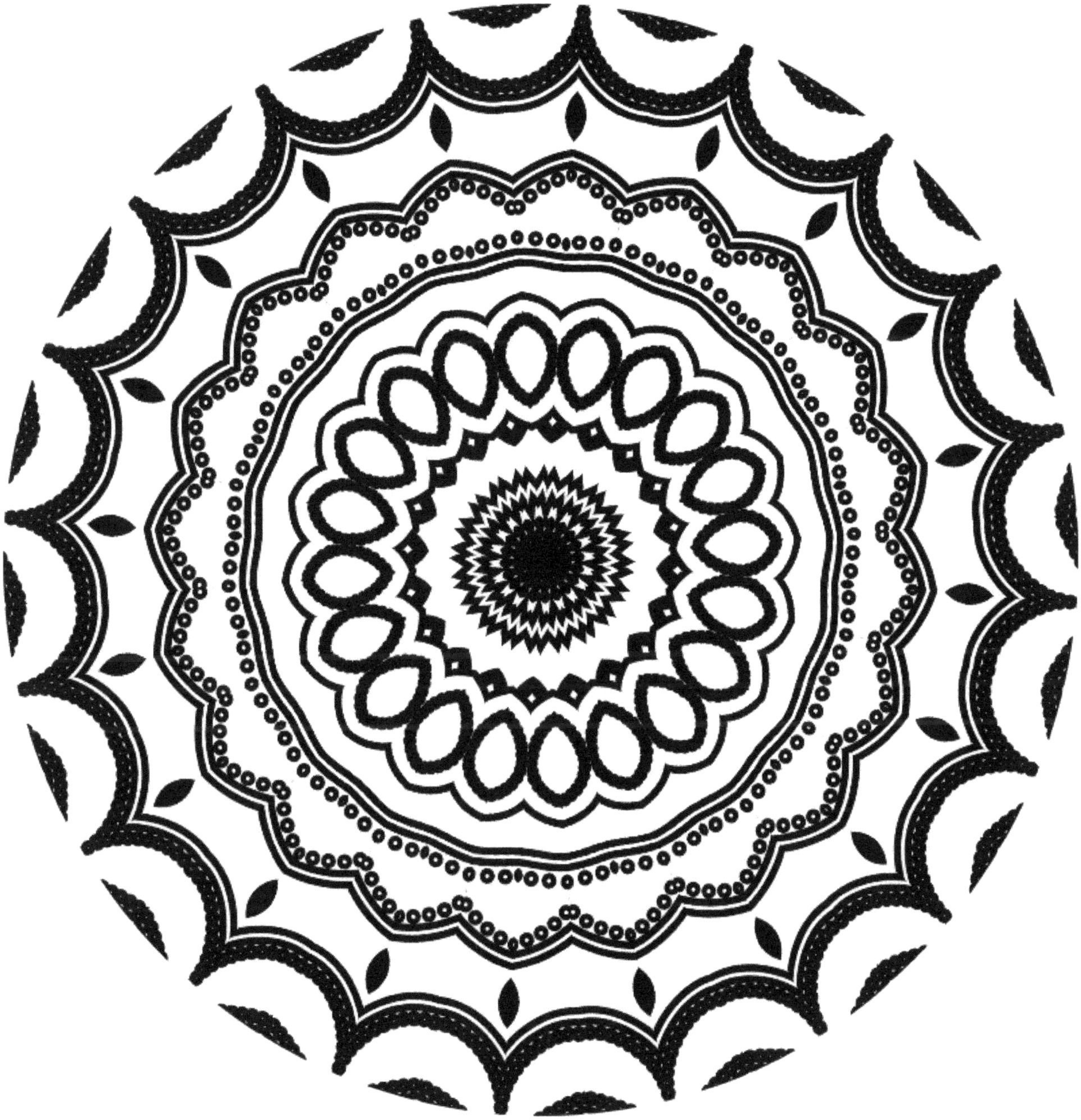

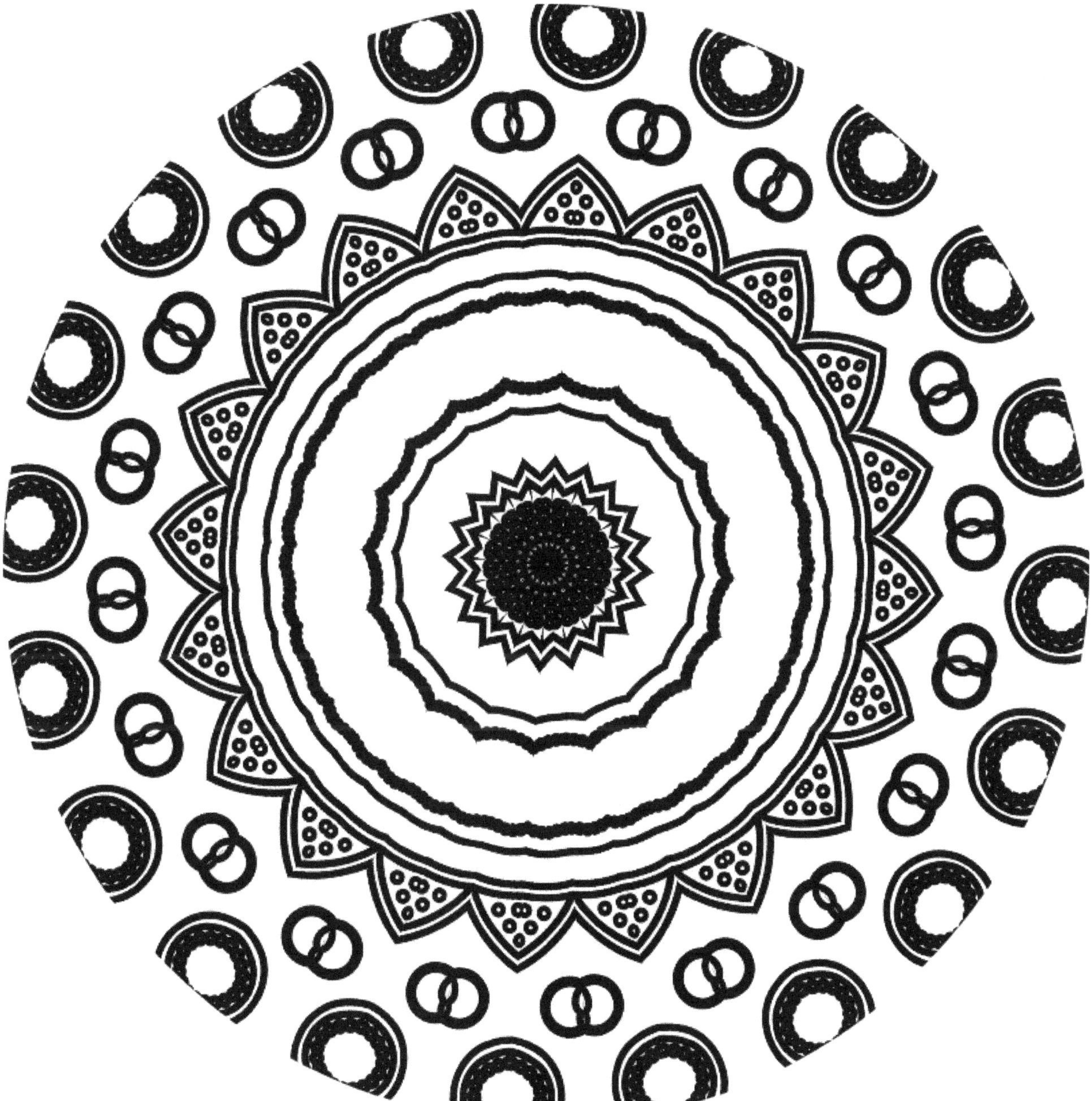

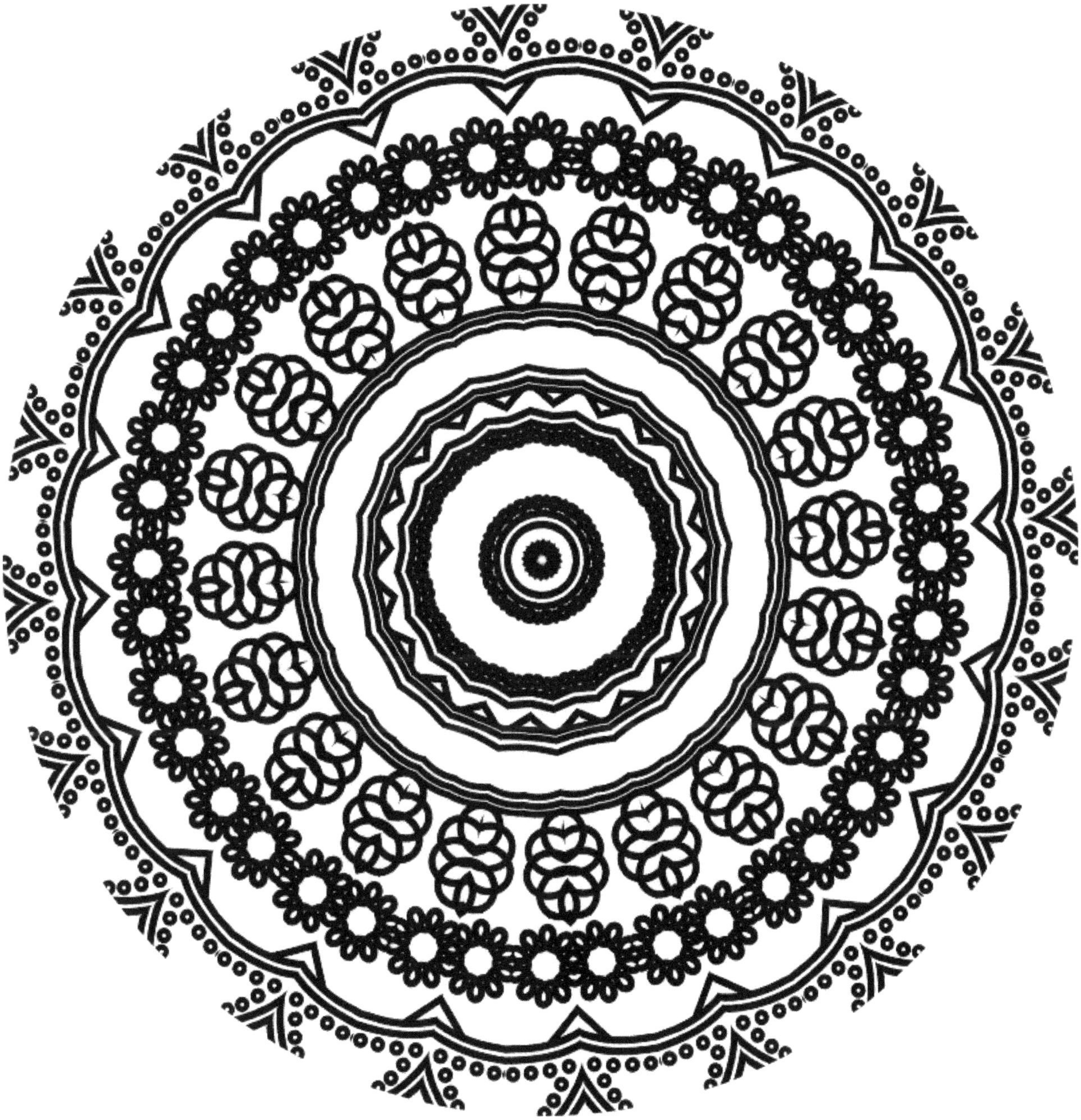

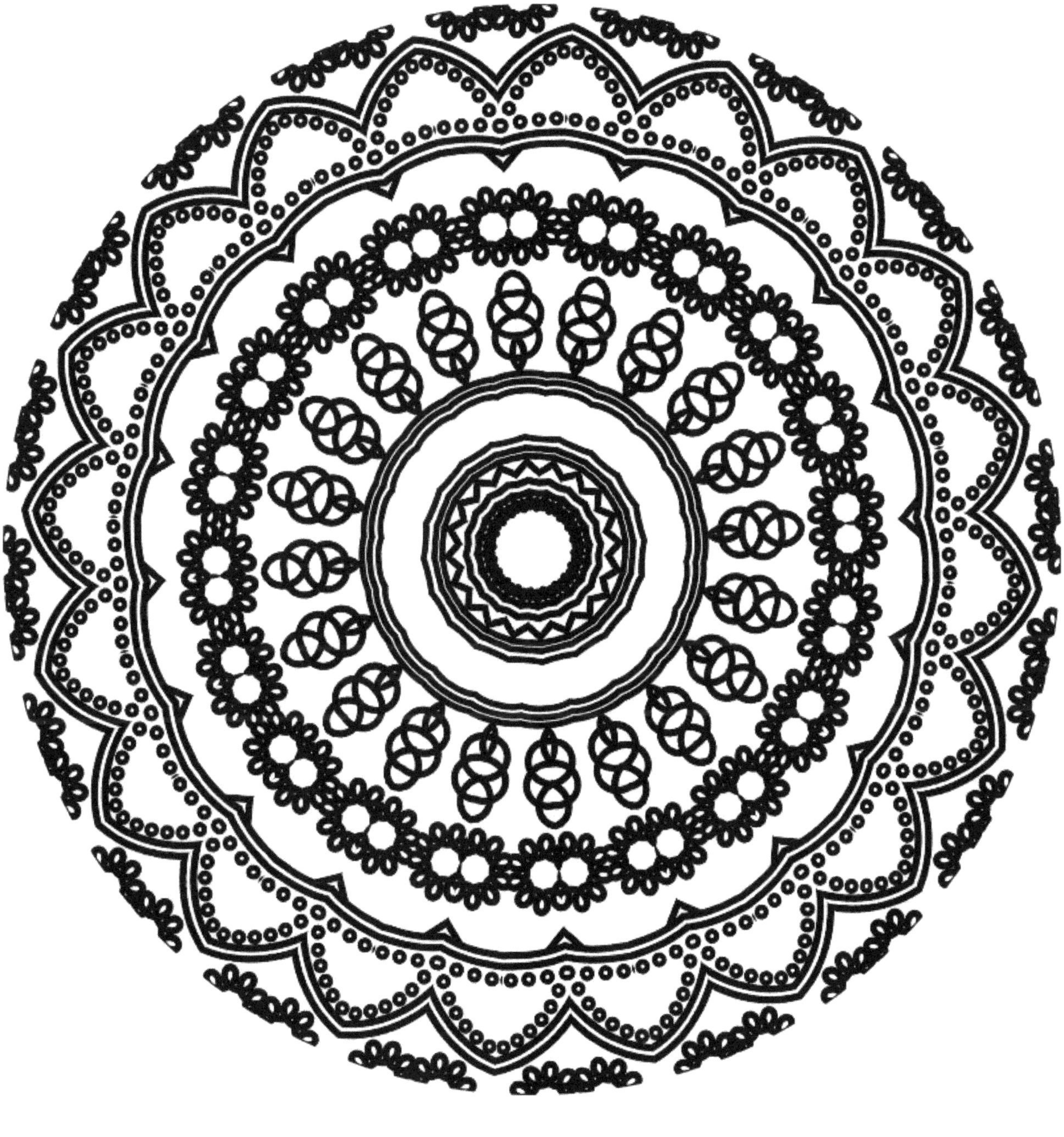

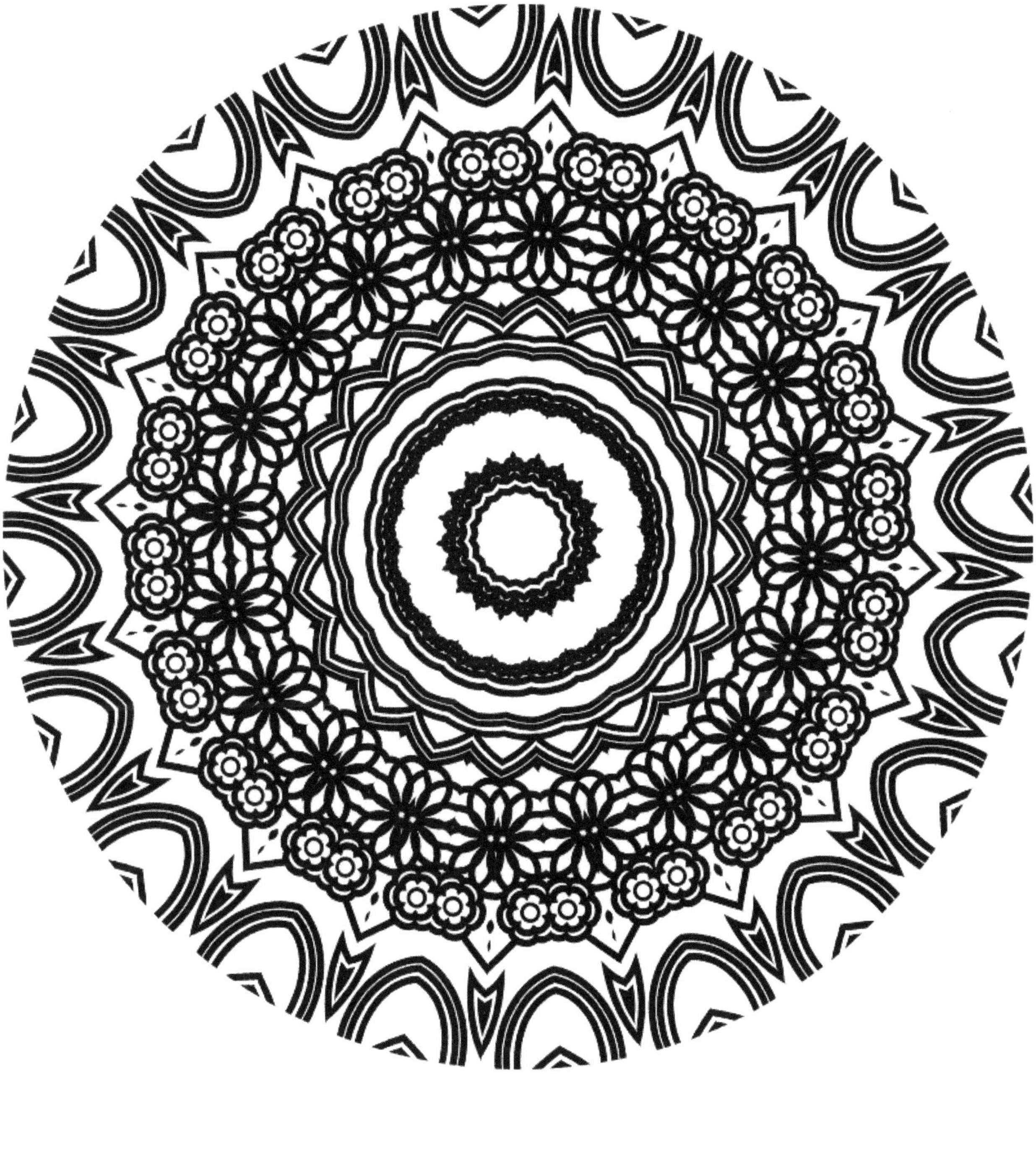

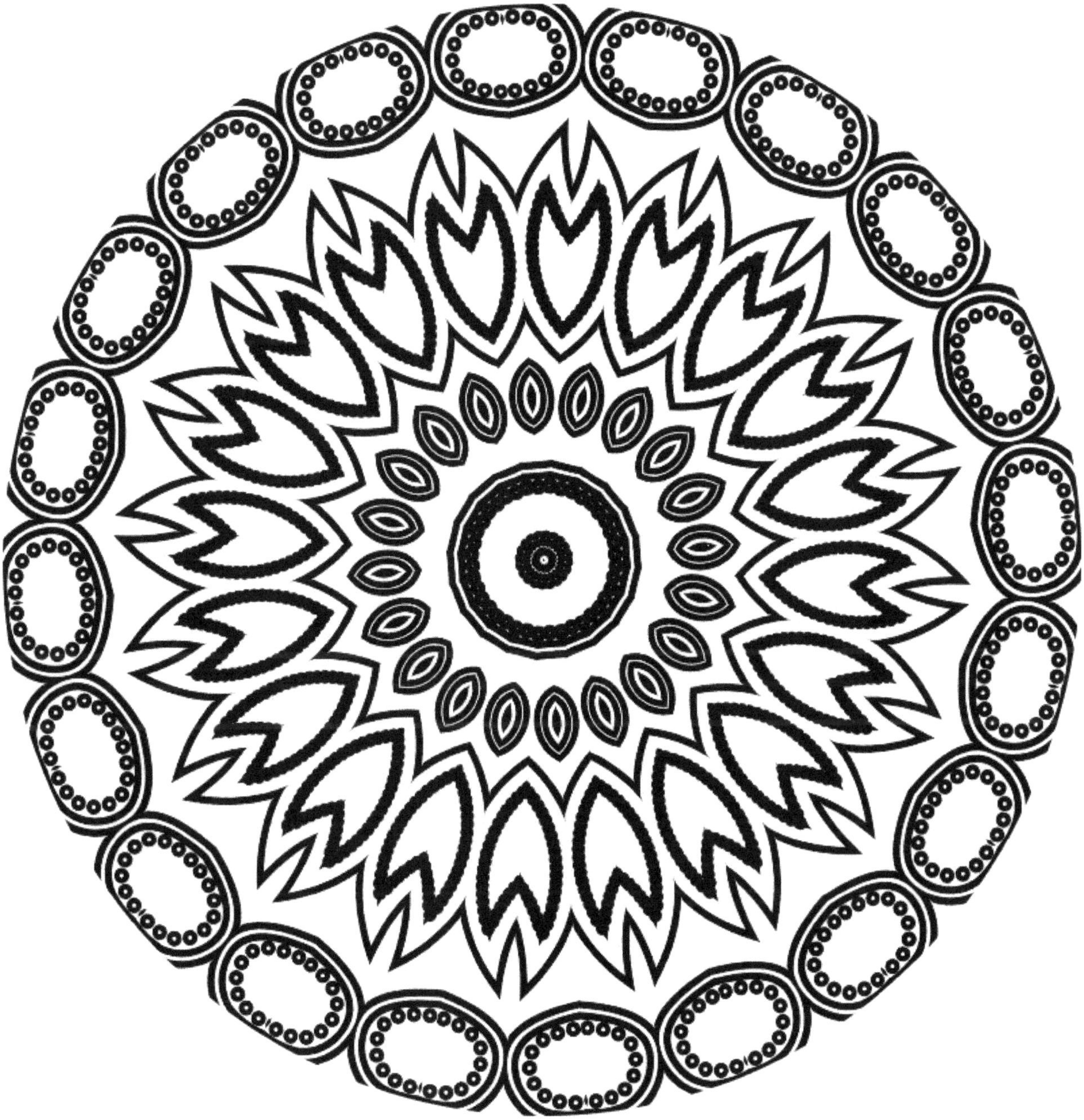

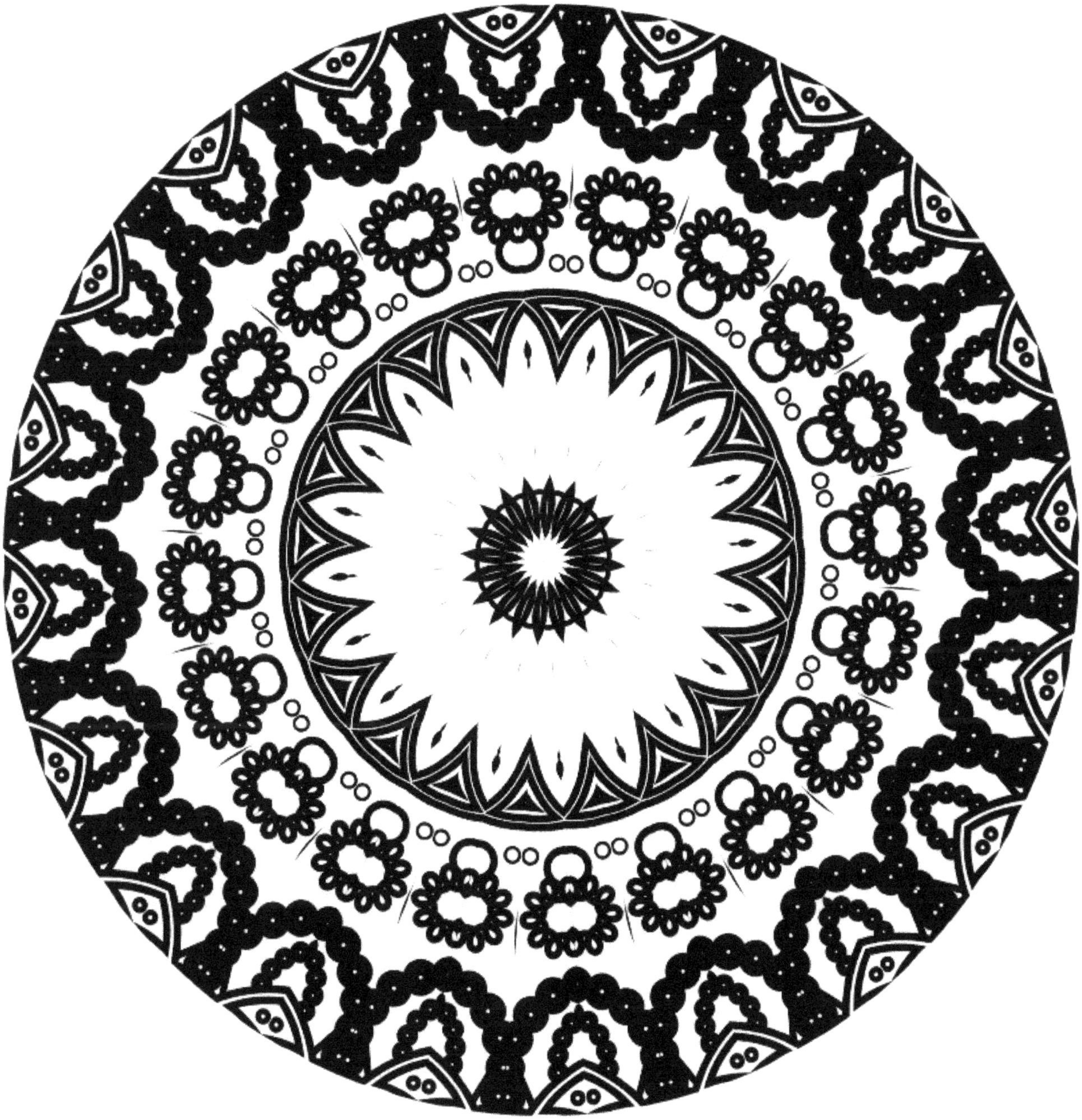

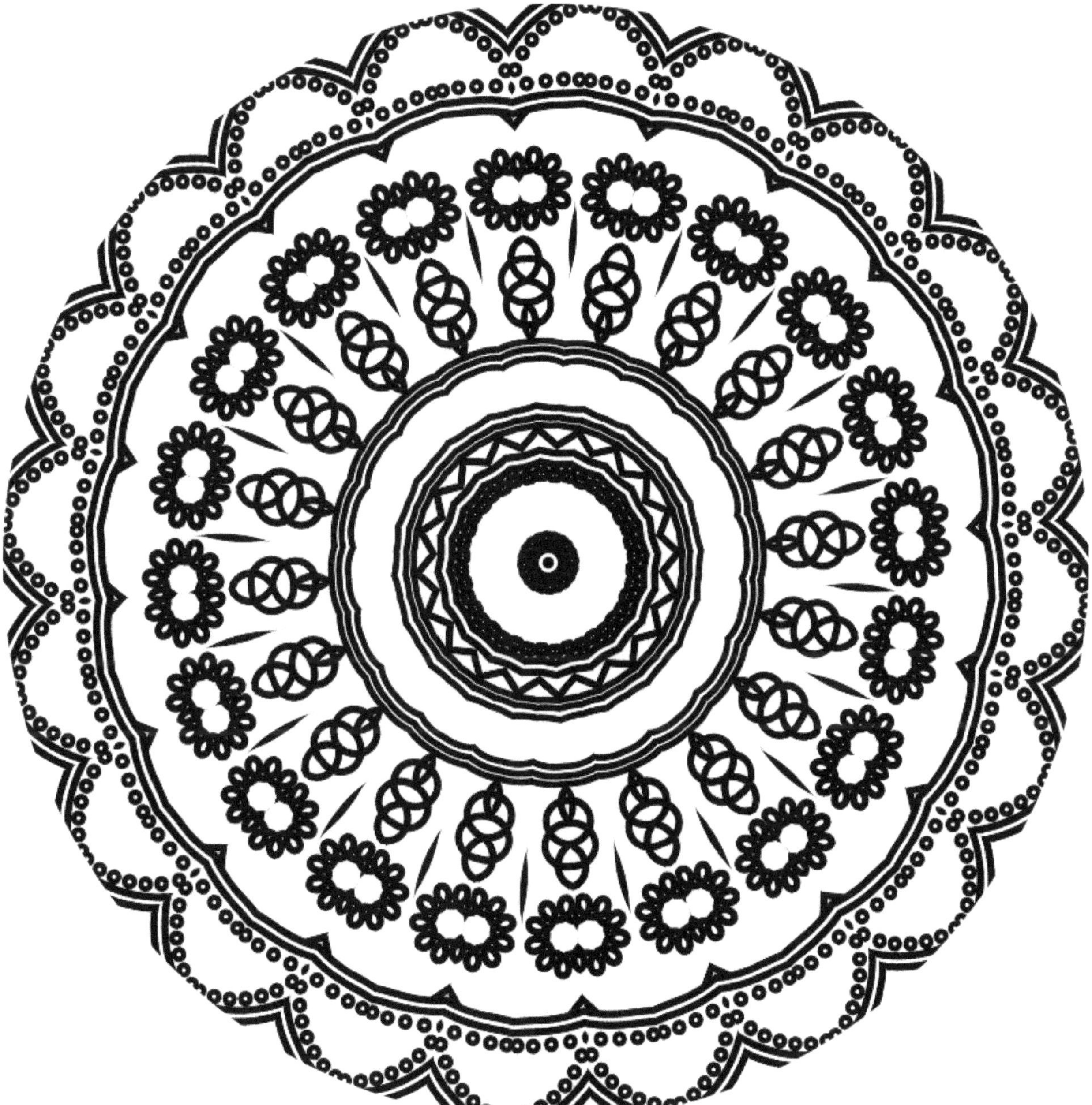

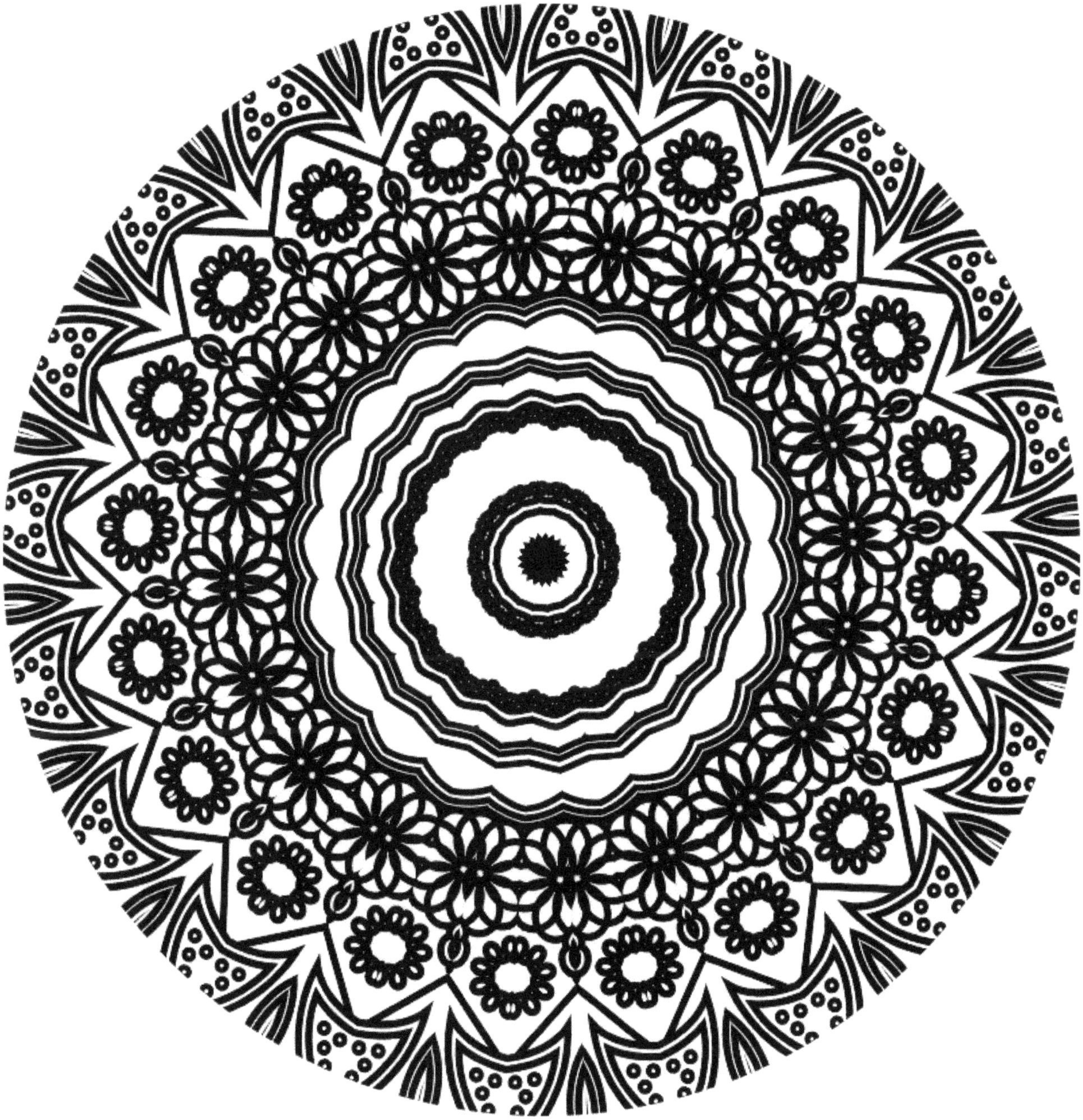

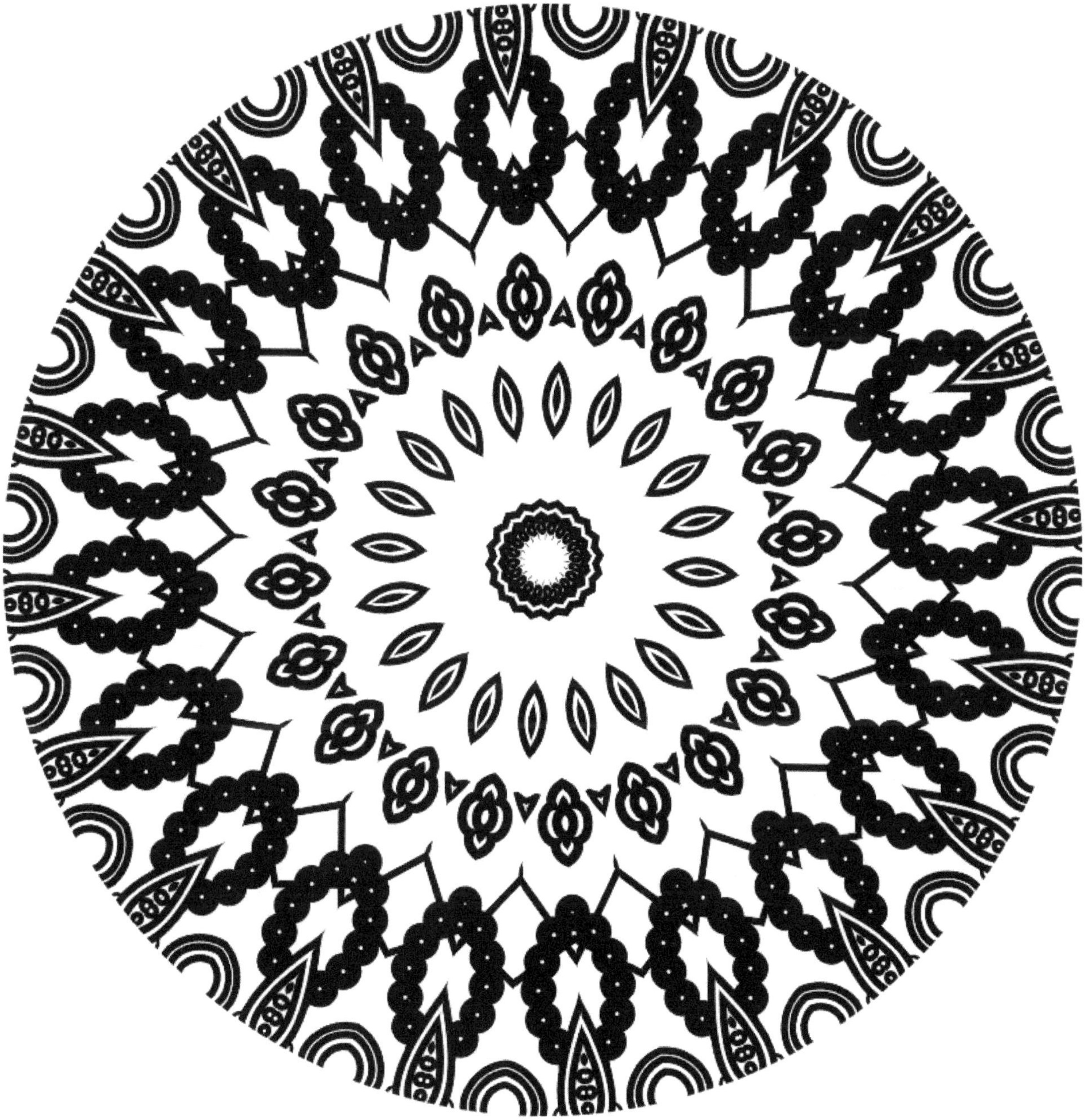

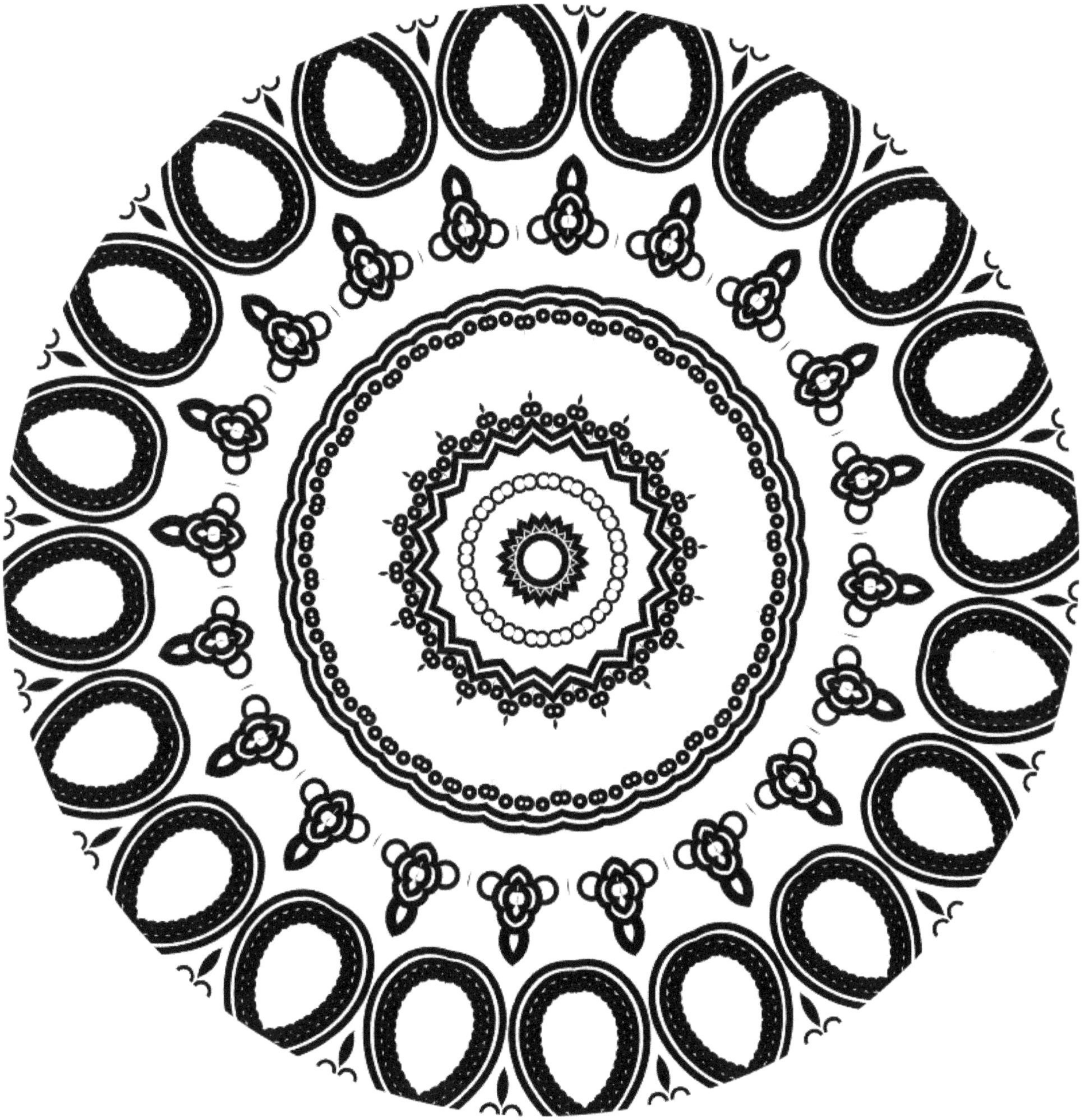

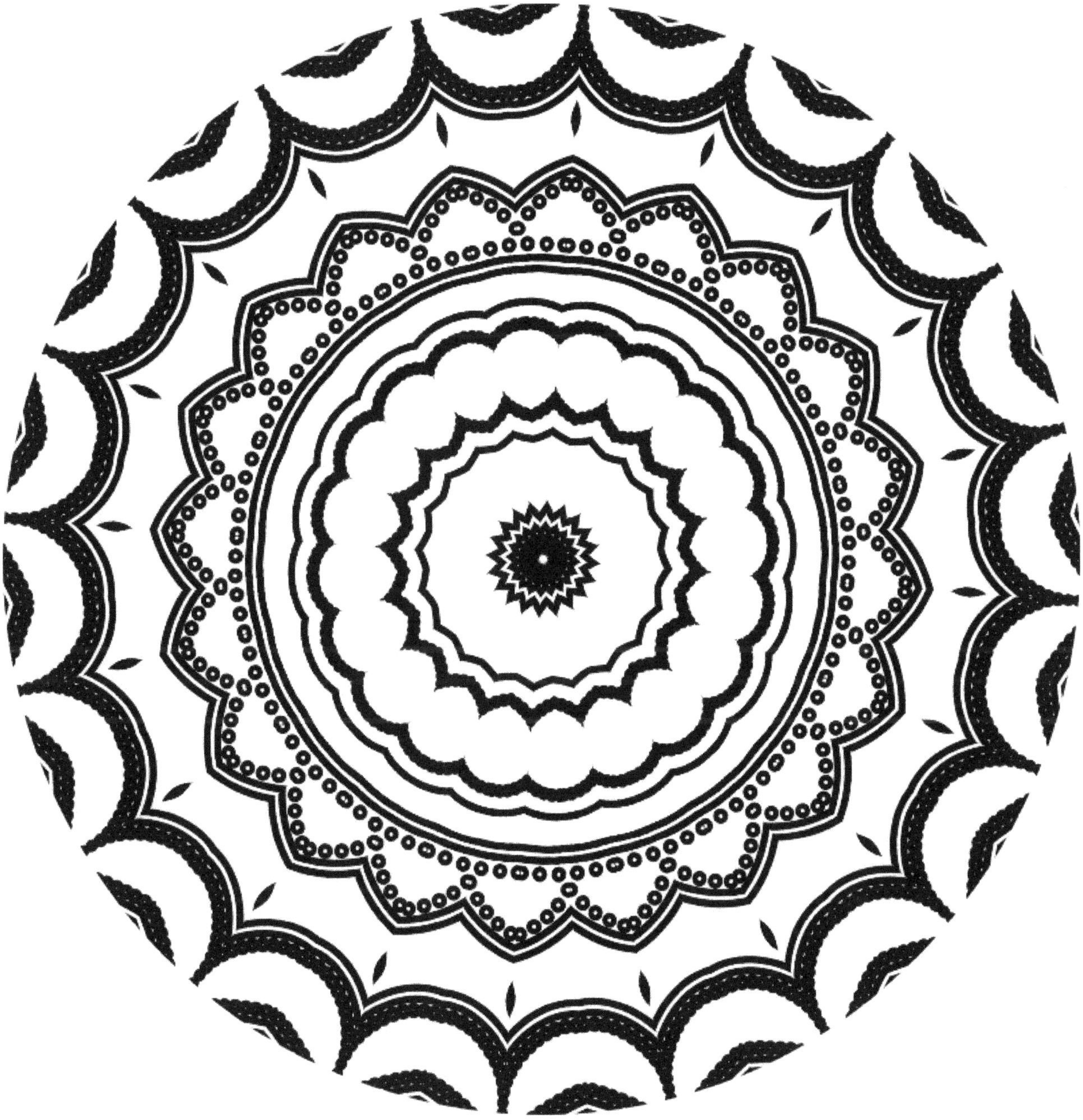

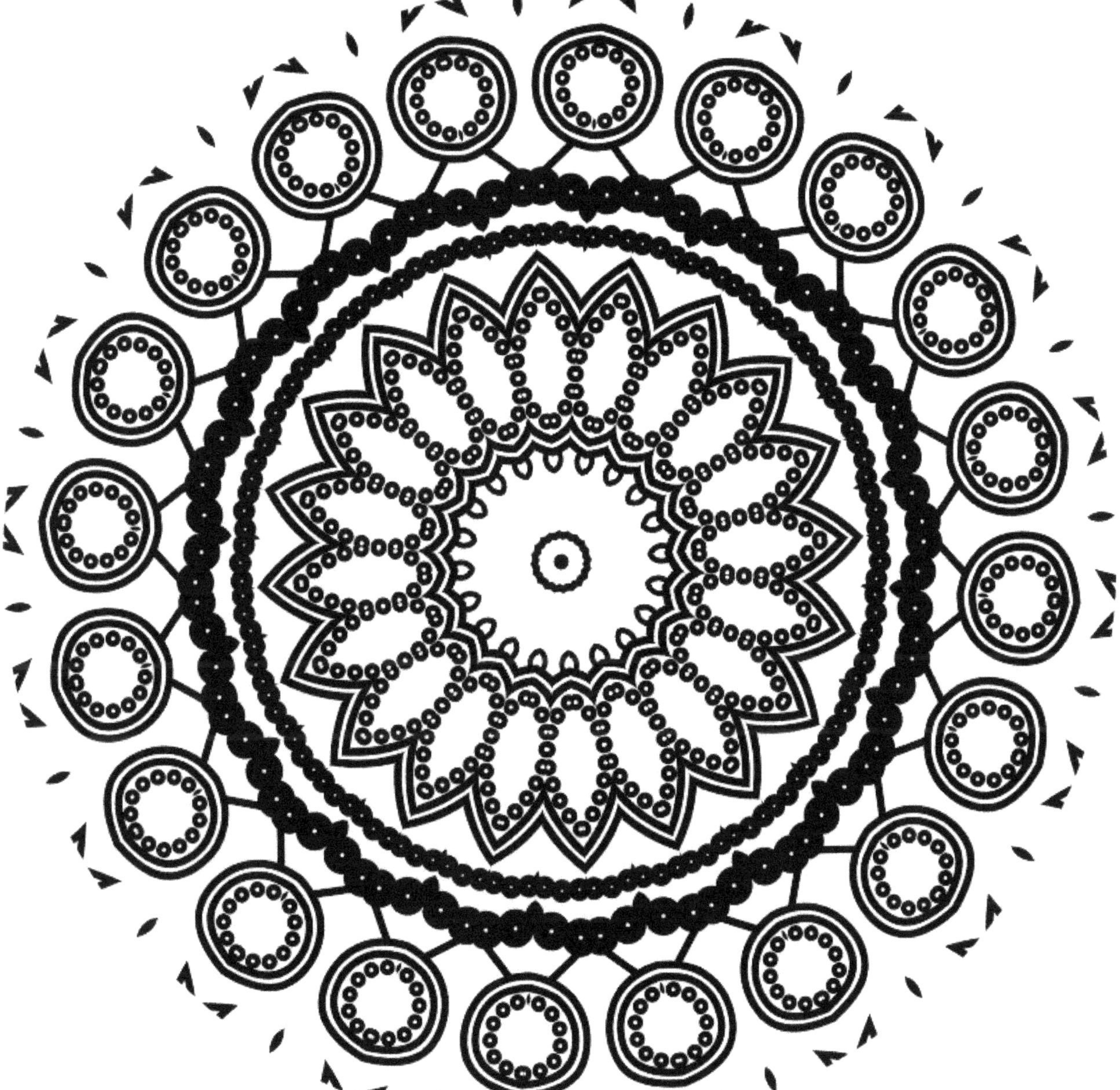

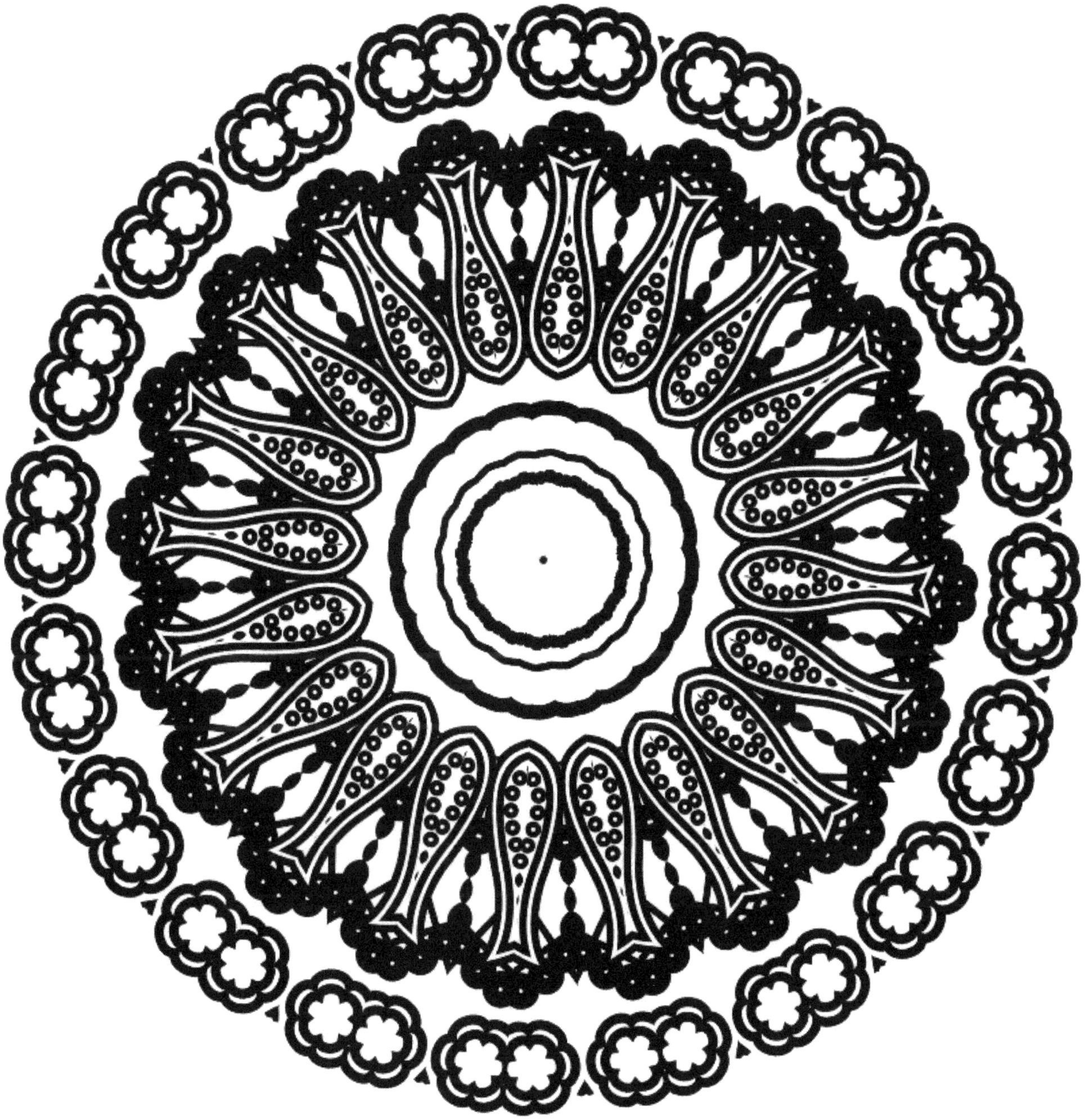

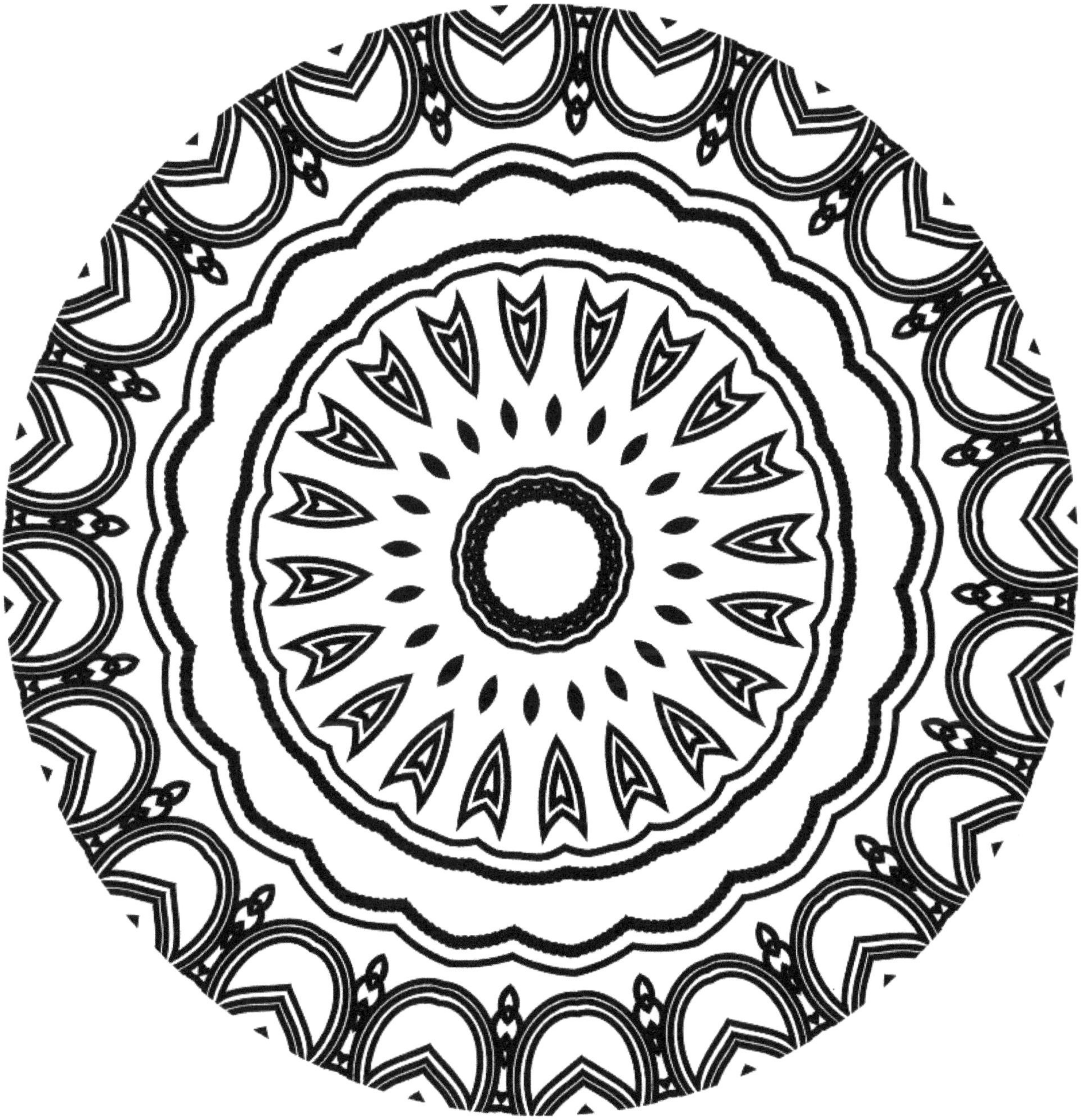

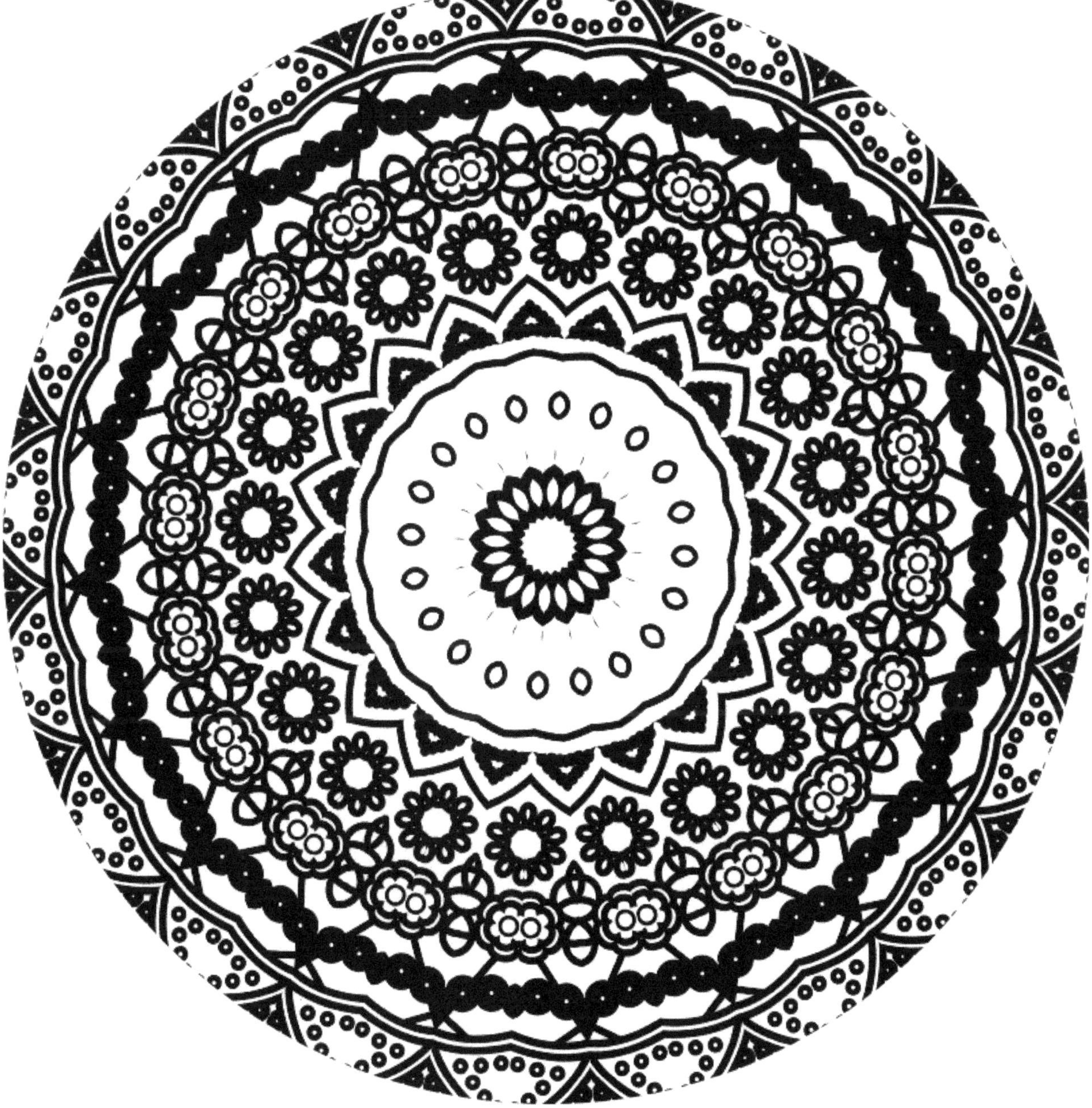

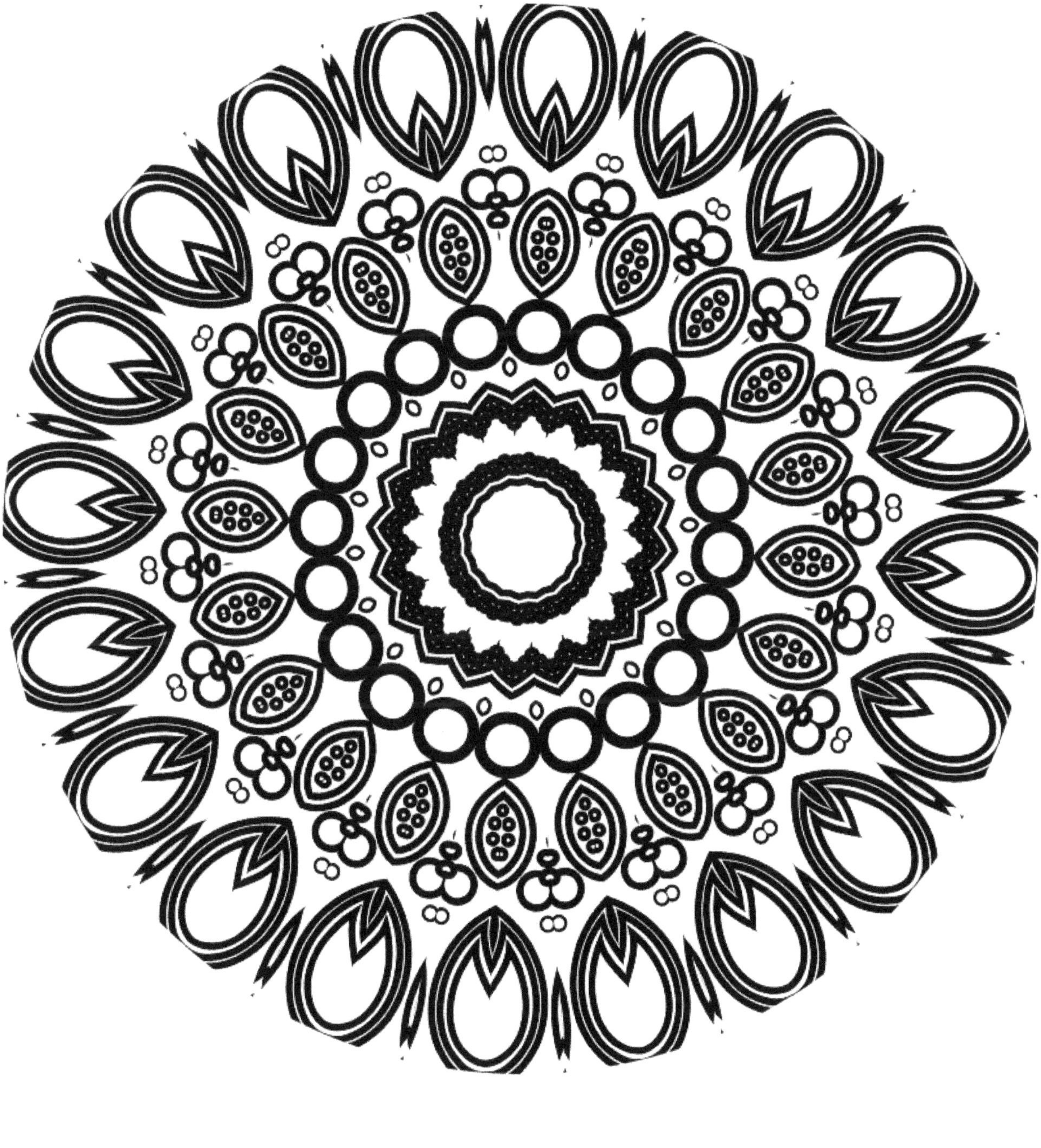

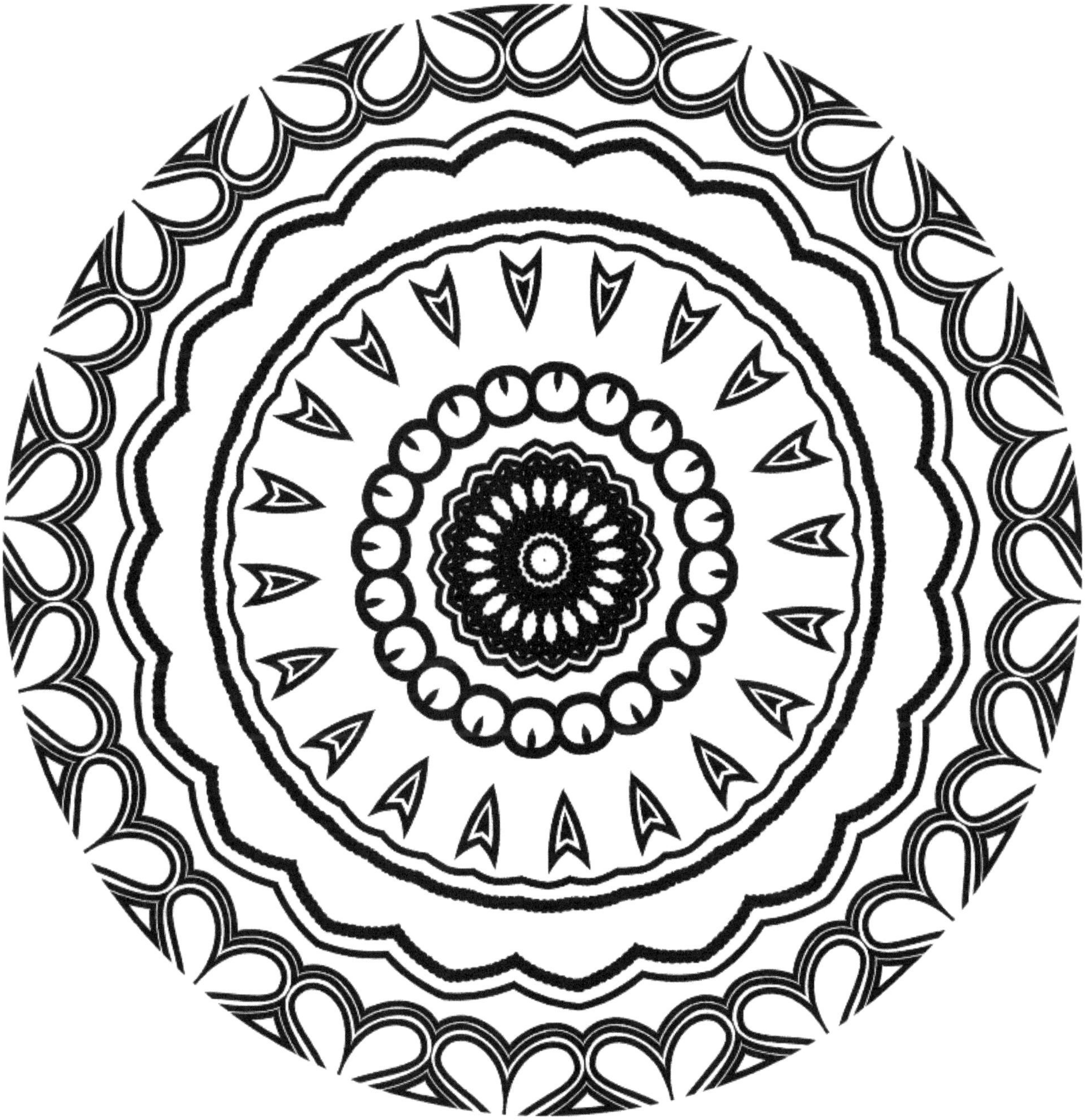

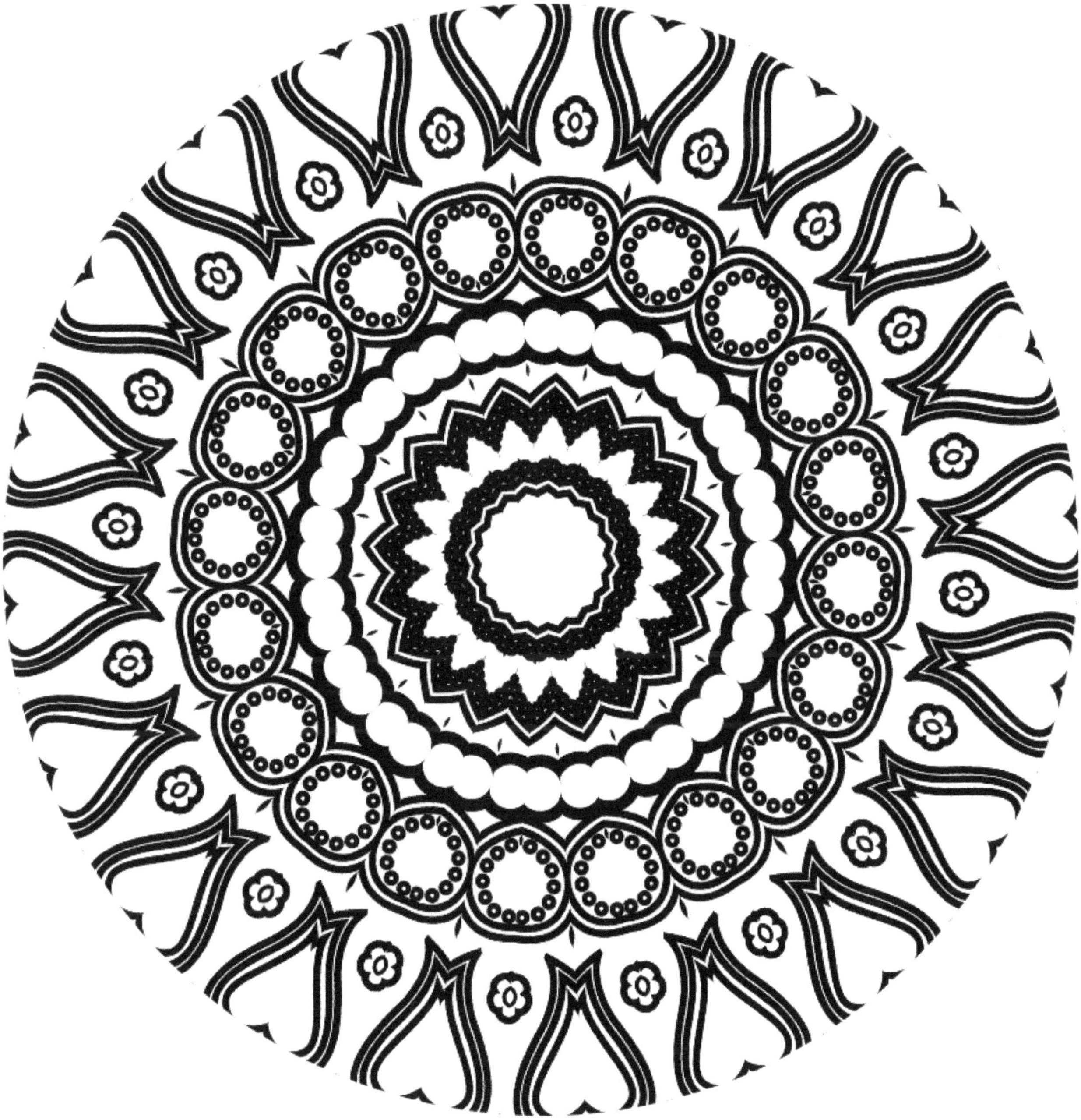

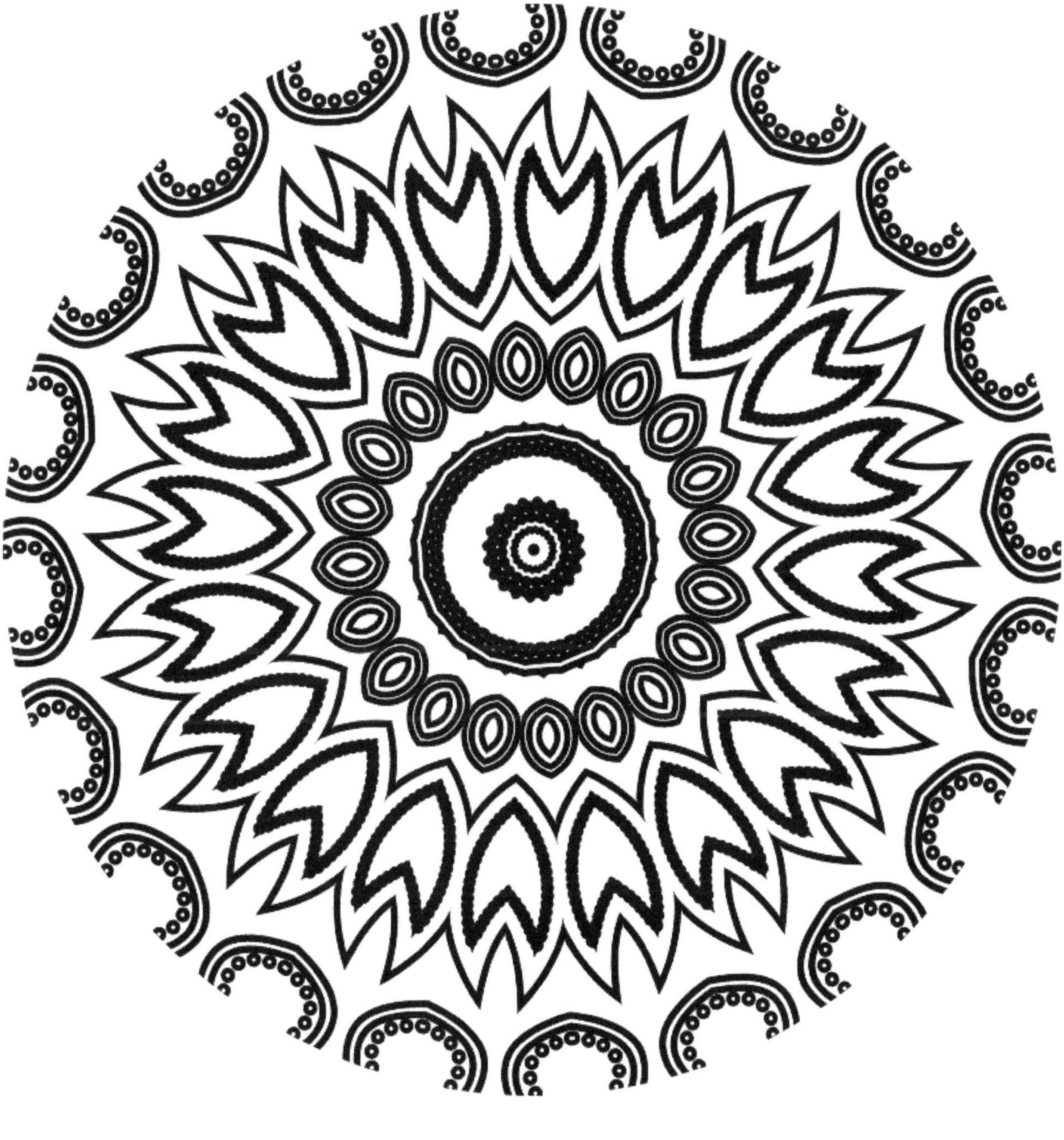

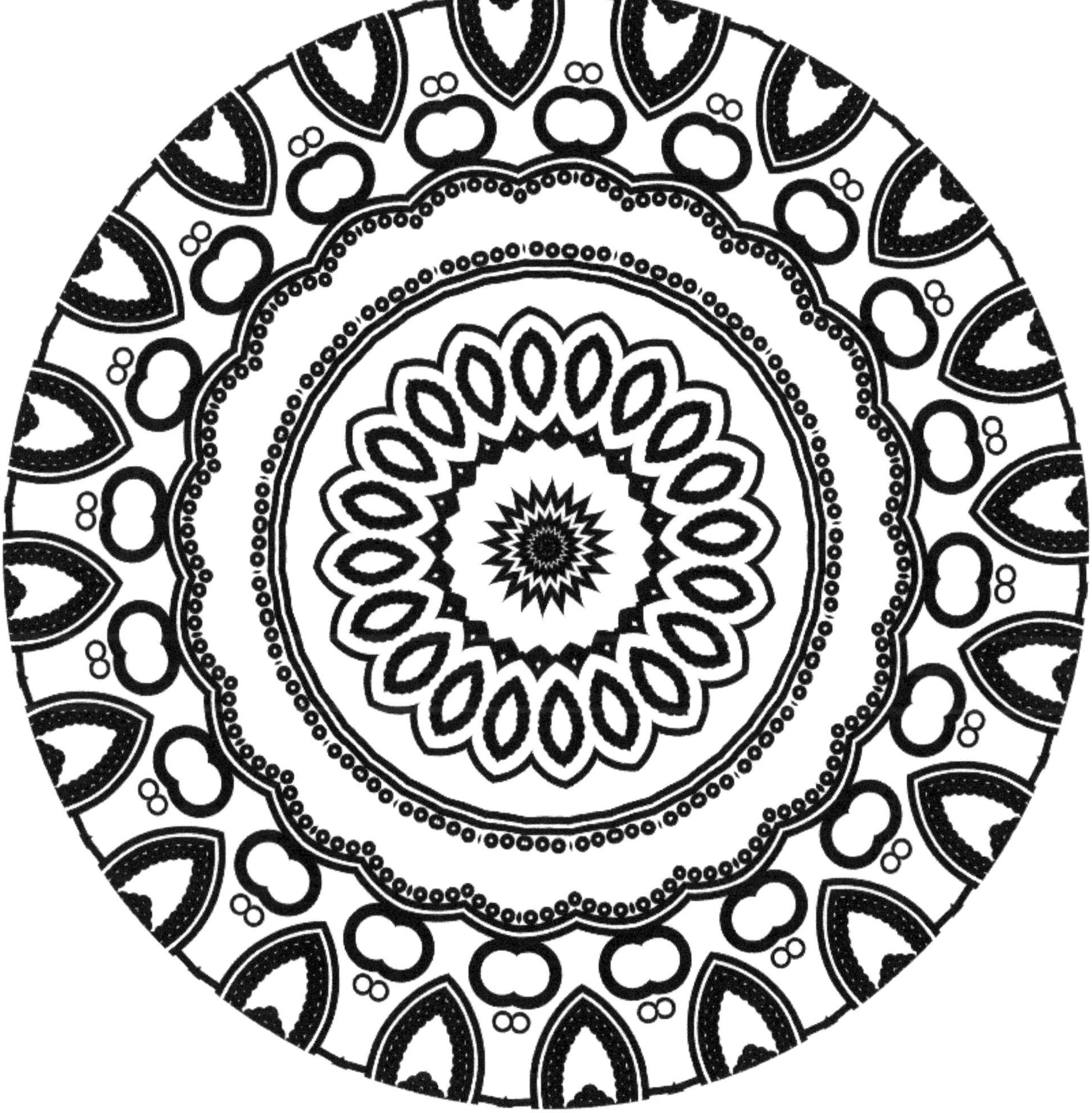